A Line Through the Human Heart
On Sinning and Being Forgiven

JAMES V. SCHALL, S.J.

A Line Through the Human Heart

On Sinning & Being Forgiven

 Angelico Press

First published in the USA
by Angelico Press 2016
© James V. Schall 2016

For information, address:
Angelico Press, Ltd.
4709 Briar Knoll Dr. Kettering, OH 45429
www.angelicopress.com

Paperback: 978-1-62138-225-6
Cloth: 978-1-62138-226-3
eBook: 978-1-62138-227-0

Cover image: A.N. Mironov,
"The Conscience," 2015, Oil on canvas, 45 x 50.
Source: https://commons/wikipedia.org/wiki/File:Conscience.Mironov.jpg
Cover design: Michael Schrauzer

CONTENTS

Acknowledgments: ix

Introduction: *The Freedom to Repent* 1

Chapter 1: *The Constant Temptation* 7

Chapter 2: *The Last Christian* 13

Chapter 3: *Humility and the "Collapse of Joy"* 17

Chapter 4: *On Original Sin* 22

Chapter 5: *The "Desire to Be As Gods"* 27

Chapter 6: *On Justice* 33

Chapter 7: *On Compassion* 38

Chapter 8: *On Punishment* 42

Chapter 9: *On Forgiveness* 47

Chapter 10: *On Mercy* 51

Chapter 11: *On Moral Reasoning* 56

Chapter 12: *On "Severe Penances"* 60

Chapter 13: *On Fame and Envy* 64

Chapter 14: *Screwtape on Pleasure* 69

Chapter 15: *On Losing the Faith* 72

Chapter 16: *On Forgiven and Forgotten Sins* 76

Chapter 17: *On Mercy and Mercilessness* 81

Chapter 18: *On Necessarily Making Us "Good"* 84

Chapter 19: *On a Cross-Less Catholicism* 92

Chapter 20: *A Second Look at Hell* 96

Chapter 21: *On Wrath and Anger* 101

Chapter 22: *On the Power of Forgiving Sins* 104

Chapter 23: *The Judgment of God* 111

Chapter 24: *A World of Justice, Mercy, and Forgiveness* 123

Appendix: *Fifteen Lies at the Basis of Our Culture* 127

You have mercy on all, O Lord, because you can do all things; and you overlook the sins of men that they may repent. For you love all things *that are* and loathe nothing that you have made.

Wisdom 11:23–24

And it was only when I lay there on rotting prison straw that I sensed within myself the first stirrings of good. Gradually, it was disclosed to me that the line separating good and evil passes not through states, nor between classes, not between political parties either—but right through every human heart—and through all human hearts. The line shifts. Inside us, it oscillates with the years. And even within hearts overwhelmed by evil, one small bridge of good is retained. And even in the best of all hearts, there remains . . . an un-uprooted small corner of evil.

Alexander Solzhenitsyn, *The Gulag Archipelago*

First that human beings, all over the world, have this curious idea that they *ought* behave in a certain way, and can't really get rid of it. Secondly, that they don't in fact behave in that way. They know the Law of Nature; they break it. These two facts are the foundation of all clear thinking about ourselves and the universe we live in.

C. S. Lewis, *The Case for Christianity*

We do not really want a religion that is right when we are right. What we want is a religion that is right when we are wrong.

G. K. Chesterton, *The Catholic Church and Conversion*

You blotted out my evil deeds, in order not to repay me with the punishment I deserved for the work of my hands, which had led me away from you; and even before I did them, you took into account all the good deeds by which I should deserve well of you, in order to recompense yourself for the work of your hands which made me. For before I was, you were; I was nothing that you might give me my being.

St Augustine, *Confessions*, XIII, 1

What a man should guard against most of all is doing what's unjust, knowing that he will have trouble enough if he does. . . . And if he . . . acts unjustly, he should voluntarily go to the place where he'll pay his due, as soon as possible; he should go to the judge as though he were going to a doctor, anxious that the disease of injustice shouldn't be protracted and cause his soul to fester incurably.

Plato, *Gorgias*, 480a–b

Acknowledgements

The following chapters, now rewritten, were previously published. The author wishes to thank the editors of the following publications and web sites for permission to reprint these materials.

1) Chapters 1 and 22 in *Ignatius Insight*.
2) Chapters 2, 10, 14, and 19 in *Inside Catholic*.
3) Chapter 3 in the *Midwestern Chesterton News*.
4) Chapters 4 and 15 in *Crisis Magazine*.
5) Chapter 5 in the *St. Austin's Review*.
6) Chapters 6, 7, 9, 12, 17, and 20 in *The Catholic Thing*.
7) Chapter 13 in *Excelsis*.
8) Chapter 18 in *First Principles Journal*.
9) Chapters 21 and 22 in *Catholic Pulse*.
10) Appendix in *Catholic World Report*.

Introduction

The Freedom to Repent

I will forgive their evildoing, and their sins I will remember no more.

Hebrews 8:12

He took all our sins upon Himself and asked forgiveness for our offenses.

Second Antiphon 2, Evening Prayer, Wednesday of Holy Week

THE CALL TO "repent" of one's sins is almost the first word we hear in the Gospels. It is a call we do not really "like" to hear. It challenges us to examine ourselves, to do something about the way we live. In that sense, it is also a grace. It presupposes 1) that we do or can sin, 2) that we know what we do, and 3) that we want to do something about repairing any damage to ourselves or others that our actions have caused. We know that it is not sufficient simply to "forgive" ourselves. We hope that some way exists for us to be forgiven that makes us aware of the seriousness of the problems sin cause us, yet something that is not impossible to accomplish.

Socrates famously said that "the unexamined life is not worth living." If we do "examine" our lives—something highly recommended—we find that many things about them ought not to have existed, but do. We would like to forget them all. But our sins, even repented ones, as we will see (Chapter 14), remain part of our own history, our own character. Our sins

[1]

define us as much as our virtues and talents do. "This is the day of fulfilment. The reign of God is at hand. Reform your lives [repent] and believe in the Gospel" (Mark 1:15; cf. Matthew 4:17). This is both an announcement to us and, in its light, an admonition. Something is now in the world that was not here before.

The New Testament begins, as we ourselves do at our birth, in a world in which sins of actual men and women already exist. Though this reality is not the whole story, we live our lives in a sinful world, "a vale of tears." The world itself is good. Many lovely things are found in it. We are to note them, love them. The location of evil, moreover, is not in matter. We are not Manicheans who think that matter was created by an evil god. God looked on the world *that* is, the one that He created. He saw that it was "good," indeed *very* good. But He was also aware of the sin and disorder in the drama of mankind. This disorder invited a divine response as the only way finally to deal with it.

The general context of the existing world was always that such a sinful world "need" not have happened, but it did. God did not intend that death and evil should come into the world, though He knew man's freedom made it possible. God took the risk, but knew He might have to deal with a freedom badly used. Once present in the world as a fact, everyone had to work out his life, his salvation, with an awareness that sin and evil are not just possible, but present. They are not just abstractions but touch every life in one way or another. We either sin ourselves or suffer from the sins of others.

Sin and evil are presumed, experienced, not merely "invented" or "imagined." They ought not to exist, but they do exist. The alternative to a sinful world, yet one within which we are to decide what we are to be, is probably not a sinless world. It is no world at all. The drama of existence includes, indeed is centered on, the possibility of free beings choosing against their own good, against God. It also includes the response, within time—within the "fullness of time,"—that God gives as His response to such sins. We call this response the Incarnation, which leads to the Cross and Resurrection, Ascension, and Pentecost.

The problem of sin, once committed, is whether anything can be done about it, not just whether or why it happened. If something can be done about it, what is it? How do we know about it? Moreover, we cannot tell someone to "repent" unless he is free *not* to repent. One can only repent what needs repentance. In spite of the witticism that "no good deed goes unpunished," no one "repents" good deeds. He rather rejoices in them. He is praised for them. This freedom to repent follows from first putting into existence an identifiable personal act, a sin, for which one needed to atone. The act that needed atonement did not "need" to happen in the first place. That is, some deed or word came into existence through the deliberate action of an individual human being. Though he could have chosen otherwise, he decided to put it into existence anyhow. In this sense, he is the technical "origin" or cause of this act. It remains with him as an aspect of *what he is*. Thus, the sinner must have had some knowledge of what he was doing, along with the possibility of his not doing it. Even when something like a hurricane or storm in nature destroys many lives, we still often look for human culprits whom we make responsible for not anticipating or providing for the emergency. In short, we cannot easily bear to live in a purposeless world. In lieu of finding some human agency, God is often held responsible for any evil that occurs. Of course, God is "responsible" for the normal workings of nature, for its being what it is. Human sin is seen against the background of natural disasters. The former is voluntary, the latter are not.

The first step in thinking of the forgiveness of sins, then, is to consider what to do or what not to do; what can be done, what cannot be done about them. The older legal notion of an "act of God," in referring to an earthquake or a volcano eruption, was designed not so much to "blame" God as to explain that not every destructive or happy event is the result of human choices. Once such events happen, we then have to decide what to do about their consequences. It is not only wrong to do something wrong, but wrong not to do something we ought to do. Or, to say the same thing positively, we should do what we ought to do, though we "need" not.

We need next to look at the action or inaction that follows from our consideration of what is to be done. Finally, the visible consequences of what we do follow. We are to be observed and judged. We need to know the effects of our actions on others and on ourselves. Some thinkers will argue that the law itself or any prohibition is itself what causes evil to exist. (St. Paul touched on this.) That is, if no law or norm existed, no evil would be possible. But law is a norm that is designed to instruct us on what to do or not do. It has appropriate sanctions for its breaking (as discussed in Chapter 8). These are designed to indicate the seriousness of the law and the penalty for breaking it. The breaking of a good law causes harm and inconvenience to many others.

When we read in Hebrews that our evil-doing can be forgiven by God, it adds that He will not remember it (discussed in Chapter 14). Nothing quite so clearly illuminates God's view of our sins as this promise that they will not be "remembered." There are certain conditions for this not-remembering, but it is the fact of forgiveness that astonishes us, and is an abiding theme in this book.

Sin does not exist in a deterministic world (Chapter 17). In a world without freedom, we cannot really "complain" about what happens through our own instrumentality. It would be like complaining that the sun rises in the morning or that the ocean has waves. There is nothing we can do about it. It does not fall under our power. Our past sins are like this also. Once they, or anything else, happen, it remains the same forever.

But there is a difference. And this is where memory, justice, hell, mercy, compassion, punishment, repentance, forgiveness, and penance come in—if sins are not to be "remembered." This passage from Hebrews does not mean that we need not remember the fact that we put a sin into reality. The point is that its disorder will not be "remembered" if it is acknowledged as a disorder, not a virtue, if the sinner restores the order he has broken.

In the Book of Lamentations, we read: "For the Lord's rejection does not last forever; / Though He punishes, He takes pity, / in the abundance of His mercies; / He has no joy in afflicting / or grieving the sons of men" (3:31–33). The Lord rejects sin, but not forever. He is open to repairing the damage of our evil acts. Both punishment and pity belong to a consideration of sin. Punishment indicates more or less how serious the fault is. Pity shows how we feel or react to the sufferings of another, even if they are legitimately imposed for something definitely wrong. A familiar Old Testament theme is that God takes no pleasure in affliction or death. He does not enjoy watching anyone suffer, even justly. But this fact does not mean that punishment and death, as such, are evil. At their best, they are proper reactions to evil acts that we put into existence.

Punishments, as Plato said, are also signs that give us occasion to recognize the wrongness of our acts. We show this awareness by the way we accept just punishment. It is quite possible for God to "forget" our sins in some final sense even if we still may have legally to be punished for them. Such punishment can be "pardoned" (clemency), but only if the pardon does not imply that nothing was wrong with the act in the first place.

This book is written with the awareness that many deeds that were once said to be sins are now considered to be "rights," "duties," or even "virtues." Much of the natural law has been overturned to be replaced by law and punishment imposed by the positive or civil law alone. Often in this latter sense, there is less forgiveness and little pity. We have replaced a system of law and morals based on reason with one based on will. We have done this in order to deny that certain sins are evil. Ironically, compassion and mercy have been the instruments of this inversion (as discussed in Chapters 7, 13, 16). This book is not a manual of sins, or a guide to contrition. It is rather a consideration of the very possibility of forgiveness in a world that sees little need of it. The alternative to a world in which forgiveness is possible is, as we are rapidly learning, one in which it isn't.

Chapter 1

The Constant Temptation

This is a *constant temptation* on the journey of faith to avoid the divine mystery by constructing a *comprehensible god* who corresponds with one's own plans, one's own projects.

Benedict XVI, Audience of June 1, 2011

THE NOTION OF a "comprehensible god" is an intriguing one. We only admit a god we can understand. The Catholic view of God is not that we can know nothing about God, but that what we know is remarkably less than what is to be known. The mystery of the Christian God is not how little we know of Him, but how much more there is to know even when we know a considerable amount, including what He has revealed to us. We are not skeptics, but we are careful. We consider the question of whether God has revealed anything of Himself to us over and above what we might know by our own reasonings. We find that indeed a rather considerable amount of what God is and is not like has in fact been made known to us in revelation. Yet, we must put this knowledge in place, in order. The relatively little that we do know of God, as Aristotle said, is worth all our efforts.

God did not reveal everything we need to know about everything or anything. He expects us to figure out many things by ourselves. Indeed what was made known to us through revelation was for our own good. We were told things about God that are to help to us in reaching Him. The reaching of God was itself the purpose of our creation and subsequent redemption. It was the purpose of the Resurrection and eternal life.

Aquinas tells us that we were a given clearer idea of God's inner being with revelation. Beyond what we could figure out by ourselves, we were provided with further insight into what was right and wrong in our lives. We were told of the relation of our thoughts to our actions. Don't murder, and don't even think to do so either. We were explicitly told of further rewards and punishments so that we could grasp the importance of our own lives and what we do with them. None of what we were told about God coerced us or removed our freedom to reject Him. But it did give us reasons why it might well be God who was addressing Himself to us. We were intended to believe and understand.

St. Benedict tells us that God indicates how we should live, through both reason and revelation, yet we have an abiding and constant temptation to "avoid" this. We give excuses. We think that revelation is unimportant or insignificant. We can get along without it. We don't need God for ourselves to be good. We can set up our own good. We must find something more to our liking. We can ignore what we know of God in reason and revelation. We want a "comprehensible god." We want a God who does not make us think too much or who does not ask us to do much. The Christian God, it is often remarked, is too "complicated." He requires too much thought of us. The Muslim god is much simpler. Four or five basic rules and acts do it for everybody. God as Trinity and Incarnate is specifically rejected. Yet, as we see from Christianity's earliest days, it is precisely in thinking about the Trinity and the Incarnation that we learn most about ourselves and our world. Indeed, grappling with mystery paradoxically enables us to philosophize better. It makes us suspect that reason and revelation have the same origin.

Yet we can fail to develop, or we can reject the truths known by reason as well as what is revealed to us. Such failures do not leave us alone. We can't just walk away. We seek to put in their place something "better," something we concoct by ourselves. We think that we can improve on both our being and our destiny. We do not put it this way perhaps, but this is what we in fact are about. We come up with theories and technologies that, we insist, are better than what is promised to us. In so doing, however, we are implicitly left to ourselves. We have nothing left but ourselves. We think that we can come up with a better explanation of why and what we are. We can create ourselves. We do not notice that what we are doing is to replace a divine plan with a human one. We declare the latter to be the more important. Men will be like gods.

If a real order of things does exist, and not simply chaos, the human enterprise consists in discovering what this order means and where the human being fits into it. Logically, this approach will mean that we find a correspondence between our mind and existing things, almost as if the two things, mind and being, belonged together. Thus, we begin with a capacity to know. We do not give ourselves this capacity. It is already there. It is not something we can set aside.

But we do not actually know anything until we begin either haphazardly or systematically to observe, reason, and reflect on things that are really there before us. We realize that many things are there whether we like it or not. We did not put them there, just as we did not give ourselves our own existence or our own capacity to know and do things. We find ourselves coming to be aware in a world that already exists. We are not the causes of what it is to be human beings. This seems odd to us.

Our desire to know things is already there within us, moving us on. We did not give this desire to ourselves either. We find it constantly provoking us, prodding us to find things out. We become aware that *what we are* we did not give or make ourselves. We can look on this fact as a restriction or as a freedom. It is a restriction if we insist that nothing out there has any relation to us. We can act as if nothing but ourselves exists, so that we have no meaning or structure except what we give ourselves.

On this supposition, freedom will mean not following what is right or proper according to what is already inherent in our being. Rather, it will mean doing whatever we want because nothing out there binds us. We even have to deny that we have a "nature," human or otherwise, as that would imply some reason why we are human beings and not something else.

The second and more classic conception of liberty acknowledges that our freedom is not based on just anything but on what we are. We are already a certain kind of being. We are only free if we know what we are and what we are intended to do. We are thus free to obey the law or reason. We are not free if we simply make up whatever we want. From the beginning, as we see in Genesis, we are tempted to make our own rules.

In *Salt of the Earth*, Joseph Ratzinger remarked: "Truth and reality belong together. Truth without reality would be a pure abstraction. . . . Man is degraded if he can't know truth, if everything, in the final analysis, is just the product of an individual or collective decision" (66–67). A freedom not based on truth can degrade us. We are not abstractions.

The "constant temptation" is to assert that no truth exists because no objective reality makes any difference to us. If truth is just a "decision," it can always be changed by another decision. Nothing is stable. We usually today do not call what we substitute for God another god. We recall the warnings in scripture about idols. We are not tempted by "graven images" or by stone poles or by golden calves. But we are tempted by ideologies, by fancy explanations of things that are supposedly easier to understand than God—evolution, or progress, or utopias.

In the second volume of *Jesus of Nazareth*, Benedict brings up the question of the learned and their unbelief. Contrary to what we might expect, we often find that the more many scholars know of their specialized field, the less they know about the important things: "This combination of expert knowledge and deep ignorance certainly causes us to ponder. It indicates that the whole problem of knowledge that remains self-sufficient does not arrive at Truth itself, which ought to transform man" (207). We can have a view of our own knowledge that makes it "self-sufficient," that admits no limits outside of itself.

Benedict goes on: "What Jesus says about ignorance, and the examples that can be found in the various passages from scripture, is bound to be upsetting for the supposedly learned today. Are we not blind precisely as people with knowledge? Is it not on account of our knowledge that we are incapable of recognizing Truth itself, which tries to reach us through what we know?" (208). Benedict here brings up a question that goes against the grain. We like to think that the more degrees we have, the higher our "intelligence," the more likely we are to know the truth. But, in practice, it does not usually work this way. It is the humble and the simple who enter the Kingdom of God first. The learned are tempted by their own self-worship. It has long been recognized that the most intellectual of the vices, the origin of the vices, is pride, the one vice that is simply thought. Lucifer, after all, was not tempted by anything but himself.

Irenaeus of Lyons, the great bishop of the second century, had already encountered this Gnosticism in the early Church. The Gnostic temptation is an abiding one. It has its own doctrine that rises above anything that normal men could understand. Eric Voegelin characterized our age as Gnostic. That is, it is an age in which revelation is rejected in favor of philosophical constructions of the learned, constructions that do not conform to reality or revelation but to the intellectual's own mind.

"Do not look for anything above the Creator, for you will not find it; your maker is without limits." Thus Irenaeus advised the learned of his time:

> And do not dream up some other Father above God, as if you had taken all His measurements, as if you had explored His entire creation, as if you had considered His whole depth and length and height. Your dreaming will come to nothing. Thinking against nature, you will become foolish. And if you persist you will fall into insanity, regarding yourself as loftier and better than your own Creator, imagining that you can pass through and beyond the realm of God (*Against Heresies*, 68).

This is the "constant temptation." It is as present in our time as it was in the time of Irenaeus. It is formulated differently today, but its essence is the same. It wants a "comprehensible god" who is pretty much one's own concepts and understandings, not those of reason or revelation. I have begun this book by discussing the constant temptation to pride because, in one way or another, that is the context of all that ultimately needs to be forgiven.

Chapter 2

The Last Christian

He was known to be of human estate, and it was thus that he humbled himself, obediently accepting even death, death on a cross.

St. Paul, Philippians 2:8

WE NOTICE THAT, in human experience, temptations are often followed by our yielding to them. Oscar Wilde, I believe, is responsible for the quip that the best way to rid ourselves of temptations is to give in to them. We are, in other words, beings who sin, however much we may not like to use that word or aver to the fact. The whole of Christian revelation is framed in terms of getting rid of sins. Understanding what sin is, then, is of major importance. We can only get rid of our sins if we can be forgiven for them. We do not expect, or even want, a world in which no sin would be possible. Such a world has tinges of determinism about it. But if redemption means that our sins can be forgiven through the Cross of Christ, why do sins continue long after the advent of Christ? This continuation of sin in the world, especially by Christians, was what scandalized Nietzsche, perhaps the thinker who understood best the incoherence of modern philosophy in its efforts to explain what we are.

Nietzsche's remark that "the last Christian died on the Cross" allows several interpretations. It is a cry of disappointment. The Christians who followed Christ did not live up to His example.

We are shocked and disappointed by their failures. Nietzsche was broken-hearted, even scandalized, by the failure of Christians to live as they ought to live. He wanted to be "like" the One who died on the Cross. So, with this background, he wrote off historical Christians as a degenerate, gutless outfit lacking the courage to follow their Master. Probably, Christ was not surprised by this failure to live up to the standards of a good life; but Nietzsche certainly was.

Nietzsche's next step was to figure out some other way to live since his disappointment with actual Christians was so great. This "scandal" over the actual conduct of Christians justified a whole new theory. We have to be courageous. We have to be "noble." We make our own morals. We rely on our own power to enforce our will. We are not "new men" but *supermen*, unflinching before the sick, vapid example of existing Christians. We are beyond "good and evil." We define them. Yet Nietzsche's new theory did not give him what he wanted either. He seems even disappointed in his own theories, a not-uncommon experience. He even ended his days in an asylum.

Of course, if Christ ever expected His followers to be sinless just like Himself, He would have had a different theology than the one that He gave us. The very facts that He died to "redeem" us and that we could have our sins forgiven mean that He did not expect that everyone would be, just like Himself, sinless. He gave the Apostles the ongoing power to remit sins, which obviously meant that He expected them to have plenty of sins to deal with. If a human being were sinless, he too would have had to be divine like Christ Himself. Implicitly, Nietzsche's aphorism is itself a divine claim, if not a recognition of the divine. The Christian who died on the Cross was the Son of God, the Word made flesh. If He were not, we would still be in our sins.

In the Breviary, Second Reading for the Monday of Holy

Week, St. Augustine writes: "The apostle Paul saw Christ, and extolled His claim to glory. He had many great and inspired things to say about Christ. But he did not say that he boasted in Christ's wonderful works: in creating the world, since He was God with the Father, or in ruling the world, though He was also a man like us. Rather, He said: *Let us not boast except in the cross of our Lord Jesus Christ.*"

What does Paul mean by telling us that we are to "boast" in the Cross of Christ? Augustine spells it out. We could easily and impressively say: "Look, our God created the world." That would be true. We could give some reasons why this change might be so. Or we might say: "Look, Christ could have been a political ruler." After all, this is what many Jews anticipated that the Messiah would be. If we recall the temptations in the desert, this world-rule is the deal that Satan offered Christ. The only thing He had to do was to fall down and adore the Devil, who really was testing this figure to see who He was.

When Paul affirms that we are to "boast" in the Cross, he is, I think, telling us, however odd it may appear, that the way the Father did choose to redeem us was best for everyone concerned, particularly for ourselves. But this way did involve the Crucifixion, by no means a pleasant affair. Indeed, it was about the worst form of death anyone could suffer, not only because of its pain but because of the utter humiliation—before other men—involved. Scripture tells us that in following the way of the Cross, Christ is being obedient to His Father. He too was following a "plan" meant for the salvation of everyone.

One can find premonitions of the Crucifixion among the Greeks. Sophocles said that "Man learns by suffering." Learns what? Learns what perhaps he could not if he did not suffer. Christ did not suffer just because He wanted to try it out. The purpose of the Incarnation was the redemption of our sins, the ongoing ones Nietzsche could not quite figure out. God did not, or better, He could not redeem us without our own free participation. The Crucifixion is something we now behold, contemplate in order to see the consequences of our own sins. But we are also meant to see what we are, in understanding what Christ was suffering; to see the possibility of our own redemption.

The Crucifixion, in this sense, is an invitation to look. At what? At the consequences of our sins. Moreover, we are not looking at the Man suffering as if He is on the Cross justly. He is not justly there. Pilate's washing of his hands, however unmanly, was meant to acknowledge that no guilt was found in this Man.

Redemption is an invitation, not something forced on us. If we freely accept the final destiny offered to us in this invitation, we are to live the life of the Trinity after the manner of the Son who died for us. The "last" Christian was the Word made flesh who dwelt among us. This Crucifixion is what happened to Him by the free agency of men. On seeing this result, unlike Nietzsche, we do not run off and found our own theory of true "being." True reality is there before us already. Our response remains that of the Good Thief, "Lord, be merciful to me, a sinner." The Good Thief saw what Nietzsche did not see, though he suspected it. The better path than the one we make for ourselves is already there. This is what our redemption is about.

Chapter 3

Humility and
the "Collapse of Joy"

When mankind was estranged from him by his disobedience,
God our Savior made a plan for raising us from our fall and
restoring us to friendship with Himself. According to this plan,
Christ came in the flesh, he showed us the gospel way of life, He
suffered, died on the cross, was buried and rose from the dead.
He did this so that we could be saved by Him and receive our
original status as sons of God by adoption.

St. Basil, *On the Holy Spirit*

ANY CONSIDERATION of forgiveness must begin with a sense of
humility, with the notion that something that we ourselves have
put into place needs correction and reordering. But even if we
have this realization that something is amiss in our own lives,
that we lack the joy that somehow we think we should know, we
have to ask ourselves: "Is any way available to us whereby our
sins and errors can be not just corrected, but forgiven?" As we
will see often in these pages, a plan does exist that meets our
requirements. But what we must acknowledge is that we do not
make up this plan by ourselves. Rather we have to participate in
this plan, as if its ultimate dimensions in the Trinity and Incarnation are beyond our own powers—which they are. Paul tells
us in Corinthians that Christ did not think Himself so great as to
refuse to "humble" himself to become like to us. The word

humble has connotations of coming down to earth. If mankind was "estranged" for whatever reason, it would require nothing less than God's action to set it straight again. This way was through the Cross, as if to say that we needed to see the results of our disorders on a wide scale before we could begin to see the steps we needed to take to deal with them on a personal scale.

Chesterton's reflections on humility help our understanding here. In his book *The Defendant*, Chesterton offered "defenses" of everything from "rash vows" to "skeletons," from "nonsense" to "ugly things." Among the things in need of "defense" is humility. We all know that humility is the opposite of pride and boasting. Indeed, it is even said to be somewhat dishonest, even a vice, when it prevents us from acknowledging our actual accomplishments or virtues. Chesterton had warned us in *Orthodoxy* that humility was not a virtue of the reason, but of the will. That is, we were not to be so humble that we denied we knew that two and two were four lest someone think us swelled with useless knowledge. It is not a violation of humility actually to know something to be true. Rather, humility is a virtue of the will that makes us look at ourselves honestly and know that we ought not to overestimate our own virtue or our ability to keep ourselves from falling into even the worst of sins.

Chesterton begins his essay "In Defense of Humility," by suggesting that today anyone who defends any virtue can feel all the "exhilaration" that used to come from defending a vice. Moral truths have been debated, disputed, and denied to such a degree that anyone who defends them sounds distinctly odd. "Something inexpressibly rakish" hangs around the character of someone who defends chastity, or fortitude, or humility. Chesterton wanted to consider humility not practically but theoretically. Yet ultimately, anyone will note that, however much we may be concerned with ourselves, the fact is that we admire modesty in our friends. The trouble with pushing ourselves to the fore, to attributing too much to ourselves, is that we end up seeing only ourselves.

Modern thought often thinks humility to be a vice. Yet, "all the great joys of life" seem to require humility for us even to notice them. Humility is required to love someone. Love demands our putting ourselves aside enough to see someone else instead of ourselves. Humility is required for hero-worship. Egoists have no heroes. Humility is attributed to Christianity. The pagan gods were "mystic, capricious, and even indifferent." The Christian God, on the other hand, made men feel secure in admitting that they were what they are, not gods. There is in fact a connection between great joy and self-prostration. Chesterton adds wryly that, if humility has been "discredited as a virtue at the present day, it is not wholly irrelevant to remark that this discredit has arisen at the same time as *a great collapse of joy* in current literature and philosophy." That is to say, some connection exists between pride and a lack of joy. When we are full of pride, we are full of ourselves. When we are full of joy, we are full of what is not ourselves. Conversely, then, some connection is found between joy and humility. There has always been some tension between Aristotle's magnanimous man and the Christian virtue of humility. To the Christian, the magnanimous man, the man who possesses the virtues and knows that he possesses them, seems proud, haughty. To the pagan, humility seems weak and undignified.

"When we are genuinely happy, we think we are unworthy of happiness. But when we are demanding a divine emancipation, we seem to be perfectly certain that we are unworthy of anything." It is at this point that Chesterton's theoretical point is most visible. Humility seems to have deeper roots than we might expect; it is metaphysical. The point can be seen most clearly by examining those who frankly deny any need for humility and spend their time emphasizing their own selves. Such people bring themselves to great perfection but shut out things lower than themselves as unworthy of their attention. But if we "shut ourselves out" from something, we are unable to see it.

Egoism does not lead to knowledge. It leads to the self as the matrix-cause of all else that is not itself. Self-assertion cannot yield knowledge. Knowledge must come from respecting what we do not know as it is. If we are to know something, we must put ourselves aside enough to see what "what is not ourselves" is like. What is less than our lofty ego-centered ideas we will look down upon. This is but a version of those contemporary theories that insist in seeing everything as gender, race, or class. Nothing is seen unless it is seen in this light, so naturally everything looks like gender, race, and class and not like itself. If a man "wished truly, as far as possible, to see everything as it is," he would put these things aside. We find that we must divest ourselves of the centrality of ourselves if we are to see anything as it is, as it is not ourselves.

"We do actually go through a process of mental asceticism ... when we wish to feel the abounding good in all things." Why is there this "abounding good in all things"? Certainly we ourselves did not put it there. Yet, because it is there, we can find in this "abounding good" a good that is to become ours through knowledge and love. We see and know that what is not ourselves exists. Anyone, because of his egoism, because of his mind motivated by only himself, may fail to see what the child sees. Without humility, we see nothing of *what is*. We miss "the towering and tropical vision of things as they really are."

The "great collapse of joy" in literature and philosophy, then, is no accident. If humility is the virtue that enables us to accept what is not ourselves as a gift to ourselves, we can anticipate being filled by the love of what is not ourselves. If there is no joy in hell, it is because there is no humility there. The proud man receives only himself. "Hell is the other" is the statement of the proud man who has only himself to praise. The humble man has all else *that is* and only then knows the joy for which he exists.

Chapter 4
On Original Sin

This means that even though I want to do what is right, a law
that leads me to wrongdoing is always ready at hand.

St. Paul, Romans 7:21

IN THE BACKGROUND of talking about personal sin and the possibility and conditions for its forgiveness, everyone is aware of what is called "original sin." Chesterton said that this is the one sin for which we need no "proof." We just need to go in the streets and open our eyes. He did not offer this opinion as a matter of strict doctrinal definition. He did mean that wherever we go, in history or in place, we encounter serious human aberrations. History books are full of them. In revelational terms, these disorders can be classified as violations of the Commandments. In philosophical terms, they can be designated as unreasonable. Not everything is a sin, nor are all sins alike. But all have their consequences. We need to remember that for anything that we can do that is wrong, we can find a hundred things to do that are right.

The purpose of this chapter is not to give an elaborate explanation of original sin, but to point out that in everyday life we are really aware of it whether we admit it or not, no matter what we call it. The most common objection to "original sin" is the supposed injustice of our having "inherited" something that we did not ourselves cause. Christ said that the first step in dealing with it is baptism, as if to say that only God can deal with it. And this is true. But it is worthwhile pointing out, in any effort to comprehend what original sin means, an effort we should all make, is that the actions of others, including sins, affect us whether we like it or not.

If God is going to create a world in which the free or involuntary actions of men really affect others, then it is impossible that what is disordered in the lives of others, or in our lives, has no effect. The only way to prevent this effect would be for us not to exist in the first place. The real alternative to original sin is not a life of virtue and happiness, though this would have been possible had not sin begun nearly with the beginning of our kind. The real alternative was no creation at all. God could not create a free and personal being who was *not* free to accept or reject Him. So God had knowingly to allow for the possibility of sin. But in doing so, He also proposed an alternative to it, which we call redemption. It is in this latter world that we live out our actual lives.

"Original sin is called 'sin' only in an analogous sense: it is a sin 'contracted' and not 'committed'—a state and not an act," as we read in the *General Catechism of the Catholic Church* (#404). The fact that something is wrong in human nature is not a Christian invention, though it is a Christian observation and explanation. Jews generally do not interpret the Fall in Genesis as Christians do because it implies the need for a Savior from this "original sin." Most religions and ideologies think that this original sin is an easy thing to rid ourselves of through changes in government, economy, or family. Trying these theories out invariably makes things worse because they do not locate the problem where it belongs.

Aristotle observed an abiding "wickedness" in human nature. All travel literature, all knowledge of historic and modern cultures, any honest insight into ourselves, eventually comes around to the fact that something seems wrong near the roots of an otherwise good human existence. And philosophers who deny the existence of such a problem are usually the first to display in their own lives the same disordered tendencies for everyone but themselves to see.

One of my nieces told me, "Uncle Jim, before I was married, I had no idea how soon moral and disciplinary problems appear among children." We had been laughing about a visit we made to my nephew, her brother, and family. Both she and her brother, at the time, had children, a boy and a girl respectively, each just under two. Whenever these two little cousins met, even as one-year-olds, they were already engaged in turf wars. The boy is about twice the size of the girl, but she is the more aggressive. The last time they were together—I witnessed this scene with my own eyes—each had one of my nephew's large, furry slippers; one had the left foot, the other the right. Both children proceeded to battle each other because each wanted the other identical slipper. The scene was both amusing and instructive.

Such conflict reminds us of the famous account in *The Confessions* of how early tendencies to sin are manifest in children and, if not corrected, appear later on in worse forms. Augustine wrote:

> So I would throw my limbs and voice about . . . though truly they did not effectively convey what it was that I wished. And when I was not satisfied . . . I grew indignant that my elders were not my subjects. I was indignant too that those on whom I had no claim did not wait on me. I took my revenge in tears. I have been able to learn that infants are like this by watching them—and they, unknowing, have more truly shown me what I was than have the recollections of my nurses who knew me then.

Augustine also recalls the story of his mother, Monica, as a young girl, secretly nipping at the wine jug.

Another friend of mine has two granddaughters, one just a few months old, the other about two years. The grandmother told me that the older child does not seem to like the baby too much. Every now and then she "slips her a pinch."

One of my little grandnephews made his first Confession. He came home proudly to tell his mother that he was brave as he went to confession "face-to-face"; none of this screen stuff. Then he added, much to his mother's amusement: "But I didn't tell him everything." The family has been engaged in wondering what the secret sins of my grandnephew might be!

Still another friend told me that he has grandchildren, a boy eight and a girl eleven. They had been at catechism instructions during which they were discussing confession. The girl told her mother that she did not need to go to confession. When asked, "Why not?," she replied that she "had nothing to report." Her little brother, listening to this "confession," interjects, "Let me go in with you the next time and I can sure tell the priest what you have done!" It would indeed be easier if others could confess our sins for us!

I was at dinner with some friends. They have a girl about one and a very lively boy, maybe three. Somehow I had been talking about Plato's idea of punishment in the *Gorgias*. We read there, as I will mention again later (see "On Punishment") that we should want to be properly punished for what we do wrong. Though there was probably no connection, the mother told me later that the next morning at breakfast her son said to his father: "I like it when you punish me, Daddy." On being asked why, the boy replied, "Because sometimes I'm naughty." A Platonist at three!

Nothing much needs to be added to these accounts. We are

aware almost from the beginning that some disorder arises in each of our lives, something that needs to be dealt with, starting with ourselves. We are fallen and redeemed. We are rather amusing in both conditions.

Chapter 5
The "Desire to Be As Gods"

The serpent asked the woman, "Did God really tell you not to eat from the tree in the garden?" The woman answered the serpent: "We may eat of the fruit of the trees in the garden; it is only about the fruit of the tree in the middle of the garden that God said: 'You shall not eat of it or even touch it, lest you die.'" But the serpent said to the woman: "You certainly will not die! No, God knows well that the moment you eat of it your eyes will be opened and you will be like gods who know what is good and what is bad."

Genesis 3:1–5

THE EXPLANATION OF "original sin," and hence of actual sins, recalls the instructive scene in Genesis wherein the Devil invites Eve to eat of the famous "forbidden fruit" that grew on the Tree of Knowledge of Good and Evil. This tree was not the Tree of Life that also grew in the Garden. Eve knew that if she or Adam ate of this fruit, they would die. They did not particularly know just what "death" meant. The name of the tree defines Eve's temptation, that is, to be able herself with Adam to be the ones who decided what was good or what was evil. The Devil helpfully told her that God was a liar, that she would not die. God just did not want any rivals. So Eve ate the fruit and talked Adam into doing the same.

Much speculation goes into the nature of this "original sin." Somehow, all subsequent sins follow its model. That is, once they are chosen, a reason is given to justify them. That reason is implicitly always the effort to make ourselves the law that we follow, not the rule of reason or commandment in the particular case. In other words, it is the "desire to be like gods."

The last sermon in Newman's *Parochial and Plain Sermons* was written for the Feast of the Holy Innocents (December 28).[1] It bears the title "The Ignorance of Evil." Newman began the sermon (how refreshing to read a "sermon" and not a "homily"!) with the famous words from Genesis 3:12: "And the Lord God said, Behold, the man is become as one of Us, to know good and evil." Newman states that "God does know evil as well as good." That is, God knows what ought to exist but does not in fact exist.

Newman in fact has some unexpected things to say in this sermon. I have always understood the temptation of Adam and Eve to "be as gods" to mean that they desired the power to cause the distinction between good and evil. The "Tree of Knowledge of Good and Evil," with its famous fruit, be it pear, apple, or pomegranate, tempted Adam and Eve because they wanted themselves, not God, to make what is good to be good and what is evil to be evil. Of course, the distinction between good and evil is not arbitrary. Even God could not make what it is to be evil to be good, as if He were some arbitrary will that makes this distinction at His whim.

"One of the attributes of God is to know evil without experiencing it," Newman states. The knowledge of evil as such is not evil. Christ admonished us not only not to murder or commit adultery, but not even to think of them. He was not recommending here that we should not know what either was. He was

1. John Henry Newman, *Parochial and Plain Sermons* (San Francisco: Ignatius Press, [1891] 1987), VII, #18, 1701–08.

rather telling us not to "plot" them, not to conceive a plan to carry them out in our lives. Clearly, if we are not to murder or commit adultery, we need to know what each is if only to avoid it. Thus, it seems to be an attribute not just of God but of any intellectual creature to know evil without experiencing it. Indeed, it seems to be a perfection of the rational being to know what evil is without doing it, to know of evil, why it is evil. This view does not deny that descriptions of murder, adultery, or other sins can be alluring or enticing. Indeed, Newman's sermon is a good reminder to us that evil can attract us, draw us, lead us on, if we are not careful about what is at stake—though we should remember that what attracts us in an evil act is that part of it that is in essence good.

Classical theology and philosophy hold that God does not "cause" evil or sin, even if He foreknows its possible occurrence in us. Any knowledge of evil includes the element of freedom that constitutes its essence. Thus, God is said to "permit" evil, but again, following Augustine, only if this permission contributes to some ordered and greater good. Moreover, evil is not a "thing." No "god" of evil exists. No thing as such is evil. *Omne ens est bonum.* Evil is always pictured as "non-being." God does not "create" it because it is not being, which latter is the only thing that God creates.

Where does this take us? Evil is said to "exist" in something good, that is when something is lacking in it. This lack of what "ought" to be there has a pronounced effect on the world. Something good might depend on what is not there. If we "cause" this lack, as we can, we are said to err or sin. But the lacking thing, in so far as it remains in reality, retains the goodness of existence within it. And it is from this goodness that "good" can come out of evil. It is not proper to say, I think, that God brings "good" precisely out of "evil." That would imply that "evil" is really a "thing." God does not know evil to be anything but evil. Rather, He brings good out of the good that remains within anything, or out of an action that lacks something it ought to have.

"It is, I say, God's incommunicable attribute," Newman reflected, "as He did not create, so not to experience sin—and as He permits it, so also to know it; to permit it without creating it, to know it without experiencing it—a wonderful and incomprehensible attribute truly, yet involved, perhaps, in the very circumstance that He permits it. For He is everywhere and in all. Nothing exists except in and through Him." Newman's point here is illuminating. The "mysteriousness" that we attribute to evil, its almost personal presence that we associate with the devil and the damned, involves God's keeping what He created in existence and therefore keeping the evil in existence because He sustains the good in which it adheres. "Being the sustaining cause of all spirits, whether they be good or evil, He is intimately present *with* evil. . . ." Thus, God knows the havoc evil causes in a most intimate fashion; He is present with it.

The sin of the First Parents, in Newman's view, was to know evil without "experiencing" it, that is, to be "like gods." Indeed, Newman argued that there are certain kinds of knowledge we should not seek, astrology, for instance. Adam and Eve, however, did gain a knowledge of evil, something they were not intended to know and need not have known had they been obedient. They lost God's presence and they "gained a conscience." What might this mean? "Beings like ourselves, fallen beings, fallen yet not cast away, know good and evil; evil not external to them, not yet one with them; but in them, yet not simply of them. Such was the fruit of the forbidden tree, as it remains in us to this day." God can know evil without experience of what it is; human beings cannot.

Newman knows that the knowledge of evil is alluring and can

easily lead to action. "Evil curiosity—stimulates young persons to intrude into things of which it is their blessedness to be ignorant. Satan gains our souls step by step; and his first allurement is the knowledge of what is wrong. He first tempts them to the knowledge, and then to the commission of the sin." One cannot help thinking that what one sees or knows from television and education often fosters sin under the illusion that certain things must be known. Most justification of sinful practice begins with a plea for detailed knowledge of sinful acts as a public good with no acknowledged awareness of where this knowledge might lead.

One final point from Newman's analysis is striking. Many "boast" of their knowledge of the world. "There are men, alas not a few, who look upon acquaintance with evil as if a part of their education. Instead of shunning vice and sin, they try it, if for no other reason, simply for this—that they may have a knowledge of it." But this knowledge is not neutral; it now includes the act. It is no longer simply "knowledge" but the cunning knowing that results from sin. Such sin makes us unable to see ourselves or to see the truth. "And having given in to sin themselves, they have no higher principles within them to counteract the effect of what they see without; and their notions of man's nature, capabilities, and destinies, are derived from, and are measured by, what goes on in the world, and accordingly they apply all their knowledge to bad purposes." The sin lowers the sights.

Newman is strikingly attentive to the dangers implicit in certain kinds of knowing. He is quite concerned about an overly detailed study of heresy, or about those whose concept of Christianity consists in a detailed description of their personal sins. "But these men, far from rising to the aspiration after perfection, do not advance in their notion of spiritual religion beyond the idea of declaring and lamenting their want of it. Confession is with them perfection; nay, it is almost the test of a Christian, to be able to discourse upon his inward corruption." I doubt that this passage is an implicit attack on Augustine's *Confessions,* the very purpose of which was not to dwell on his sins themselves but to aspire after perfection. Newman's effect here is to remind us that Christianity is only indirectly about sin and evil. It is about what is good, about eternal life. Too much "confession," too much attention to the sequence of disorder in the soul often becomes a handbook for "how to sin." Newman does remind us that to be "ignorant of evil," something that at first sounds so undramatic, is in fact the way we are intended to live. We are to know what evil is, without having learned it by doing it. In the end, what is really interesting is not sin, or that it can be forgiven, important as that is. The great adventure is to know *what is,* what is good.

Chapter 6
On Justice

Then we must suppose that the same is true of a just person who falls into poverty or disease or some other apparent evil, namely that this will end well for him, either during his lifetime or afterwards, for the gods never neglect anyone who eagerly wishes to become just and who makes himself as much like a god as a human can by adopting a virtuous way of life.

Socrates, *The Republic*, 613a

This is he whom we once held as a laughingstock and as a type for mockery, fools that we were! His life we accounted madness, and his death dishonored. See how he is accounted among the sons of God; how his lot is with the saints! We, then, have strayed away from the way of truth, and the light of justice did not shine for us.

Wisdom 6:3–6

IF WE SPEAK of forgiveness, it is well to clarify it by talking about the way we live. Logically, if nothing that we do needs forgiveness, then we have no problem. But most of us do have things, some small, others large, that need to be forgiven. Justice, we saw, concerns our relations with others. Am I just to others? The vice of injustice likewise implies that we put in the world an act that lacks something that ought to be there; it lacks justice, in other words. People complain about these questionable acts of ours. They tell us about their disorder.

Many parents have observed that almost the first moral

inkling their children manifest as they grow is about justice. They insist that something is "mine." One will accuse his siblings of taking "my" candy or "my" toy. From the beginning, a child distinguishes between mine and thine. Appeals are made to parents to right the wrong as if there is a real difference between them. Yet, if someone, child or adult, does violate something just or fair, he needs not only to restore justice but to indicate some sorrow or compunction. He wants to be allowed back into the good graces of others by being forgiven.

Cities and law courts were originally set up so that justice could be established among both friends and strangers. Feuds revealed that issues of justice were being solved merely by personal force. It was quickly discovered that both parties to a dispute over some property or contract saw things with their own eyes. The law court was set up to be a neutral judge between the two parties, a place where passion was replaced by reason. Law enforcement agencies were set up to enforce the court's decision. Both disputing parties would agree or be required to accept the judgment of the law, even if its judgment was not in their favor. This delicate balance was accepted only so long as the law and the judges were themselves considered to be fair and prudent, not themselves unjust. An unjust judge made living together peacefully even more difficult. If we had justice, it was hoped, we would not have conflict. But this hope, as we have seen in the previous chapter, still had to take account of the consequences of original sin in our lives. The tendency to choose against the law, to make our own laws, did not cease even when we knew what justice is and sought to put it into practice.

The just man, Socrates said, strives to make himself as virtuous as the gods. But Plato himself worried that the world was not made in justice. Indeed, he thought that it was quite obvious that many good deeds were unrewarded in the courts of most cities and in the lives of most men. Likewise, many crimes and heinous deeds went unpunished in this world in all times and places. The world was made in injustice, with obviously unpunished crimes in it, unless there was a transcendent judgment beyond this world to requite the demands of justice. And what were the "demands" of justice? The classical definition of justice was simply "To render to each what is due." This is still its best definition.

Aristotle saw that "justice" is a virtue (a habit) developed in our souls through our doing just acts. We are not born just, but we are born with the capacity of being just. We have to acquire justice. The just man habitually, when the occasion arises, renders to another what is due to him. What is "due" is something objective, something reasonable. It is something borrowed, owed, or agreed upon to restore to another. Contracts, written or oral, stipulate in what this "due" consists.

Aristotle also recognized two kinds of justice. The first is what he called "rectificatory" or "making-right" justice (commutative). This kind of justice is the arrangement between individuals or groups about what is due to each other. Distributive justice means the proportionate giving of public goods, burdens, and honors to those who deserve them. To those who contribute more, more is due. Both forms of justice seek what was fair so that no claims are unmet.

The first form of justice (commutative) between individuals has two aspects. One has to do with voluntary relations, things that need not exist but are chosen to be put into effect by men. The other side of commutative justice arises from involuntary sources, from what is due because of accidents or crime. The whole of the commercial, cultural, and economic world depends on the justice that binds people to promises. Individuals try to do or make something together that can only be done if they abide by the justice between them. Justice occurs when people know what they are to do and do it. This justice lies at the origin of the increased wealth and order of the world. When accidents or crimes occur, however, justice seeks to requite the damage. Through insurance, courts, and punishment societies have developed various ways to meet damage that is caused by willful or accidental unjust actions.

Justice is a virtue. This means that the just man judges what is right to return to others in each particular case. He has control of himself so that he actually does what is required in each instance. The passage quoted above from the Book of Wisdom, along with the last book of the *Republic*, reminds us that unjust men ultimately do not get away with their crimes. The "light" of justice is on those who rule themselves so as to be just men toward others. Eventually the unjust come to realize the scope of their injustice, even if only after this life. It appears that not only are we to be just, but we are to acknowledge what justice is.

Justice does not primarily look to the person to whom we are being just, but to what is owed to him. Justice is not friendship, even though friends are to be just to one another. Potentially, we are to be just to anyone with whom we deal, either in exchanges or in repairing damage. We cannot be friends with everyone, though we can strive to add friendliness to our normal just relations. Aristotle has no trouble in calling relations of utility or pleasure friendships, but they are not the most profound kinds of friendship.

We hear something of what is called today "social justice." Usually, this "justice" is not what Aristotle meant by distributive justice. It rather proposes that one cannot be just unless the "structures" of society are so configured that one can be just. Aristotle and Plato placed the emphasis rather on the individual person. They suggested that social and political structures primarily followed on the virtues or vices of individuals, not the other way around. No doubt, political and economic institutions can make it easier or more difficult to be just. But to propose that such structures "make" people just or unjust is to mislocate the real sources of societal conduct. It is on personal freedom and judgment that any society must ultimately be based.

But justice has its limits. It was clear to Aristotle that the strict application of laws was itself sometimes unjust in practice. The virtue of "equity" was designed to deal with those instances in which the letter of the law itself was a cause of injustice. But it is not just the efforts to be just that sometimes need to be adjusted in the name of justice itself. Much of our lives deals with issues that are, without denying its centrality, beyond justice. This is why in dealing with justice, we also, for a complete picture of our reality, need to deal with compassion, forgiveness, punishment, and mercy. Each of these issues needs to be considered. Each of them, if we are not careful, can have the effect of undermining justice and overturning reason. So each must be considered for what it is. Yet, the rendering to each his due remains at the heart of justice.

Chapter 7

On Compassion

Make known the needs and burdens
Your compassion bids us bear,
Stirring us to faithful service,
Your abundant life to share.

Hymn, Morning Prayer, Friday, Week III

THE WORD *compassion* means to "suffer with" someone, with the sense of coming to the person's aid. It is a response in us caused by some evil or dire condition seen in someone else. The Good Samaritan is a memorable example (Luke 10:25–37) of compassion in action. The word *pity* means a feeling of sadness or fear at the unavoidable lot of another, whose situation may be either deserved or undeserved. As in the hymn cited above, compassion can mean bearing with the ordinary duties and issues that come with beings of our kind living the lives that God has given to us. Compassion does not imply escape from burdensome duties but supporting someone through them with the recognition that the only way we can be what we are is to live through the joys and sorrows of a human life.

The dramatic art of tragedy enables us to expand our inner experience. Through beholding the representation of another's suffering, we can contemplate and feel what we might not experience in our own lives. Both compassion and pity incite us to feel another's suffering. This feeling of the sorrows or the impact of the sins of others widens our universe beyond the narrow confines of our immediate experience. We become more human when we know more than ourselves. Both our knowledge and our feelings allow us to participate in what goes on in the souls of others. They are not alone.

But notions of compassion, sympathy, sincerity, mercy, and pity need to be watched very closely. They arise more from emotion than from thought. Each of these related concepts refers to a feeling. It is caused by our being confronted with the dire (or happy) situation of another. But we do not fully penetrate to the soul of the other for whom we have compassion. Only God can do that. Most people prefer to be kindly and to be thought so. In Matthew (9:36), Christ has "compassion" on the multitudes, who are like lost sheep. Luke speaks of "the tender compassion of our God" (1:78).

The concept of compassion can seem to resemble that of mercy, which usually has something to do with what is beyond (but not opposed to) justice. God's compassion obviously takes up where our sins and our finiteness leave off. We can speak of "pity" for the victims of an earthquake where no human being is really at fault for the damage done. We can "pity" those struck by lightning. Mercy, however, begins where fault exists. God does not deny the freedom of anyone who refuses to acknowledge that anything needs to be forgiven.

Still, I am concerned here with something peculiar about compassion and sympathy. Compassion literally means to "suffer with" another because we see his suffering; we can imagine it in ourselves. Yet, we have to ask: "What is the 'cause' of another's suffering?" We need to do more than just notice that he is suffering. If I say that it is terrible that someone else suffers, no matter what the reason, I soon find myself separating the suffering from the cause of the suffering.

From here, it is but a short step to confuse the suffering with its natural cause. It is quite possible that my suffering is caused by my own choices or understandings. If I do certain things that are wrong, no matter what civil law or custom says, I ought to suffer from them. Indeed, I will suffer eventually whether I like it or now. Plato said that I should want to suffer for my sins. So if I divorce unjustly, procure abortions, practice homosexuality, kill, sell dope, bribe, tell lies, or steal, sooner or later, even in this life, I am going to suffer and cause others to suffer. Nature has its ways of punishing us. If I do something that is against the natural order of my being, I will suffer for it. Nine times out of ten, I do not have to wait till the last judgment to experience the chaos I cause.

But it is quite possible, even at the last judgment, for me to refuse to acknowledge that what caused my suffering was the result of my own acts that deny my own good. In such a case, I would be implicitly seeking to re-order the world so that my suffering is blamed, not on me, but on a disordered world. *I am a victim! Sympathize with me!* What compassion can do, quite subtly, is to shift our intellectual attention from what is going on, from the disordered cause, to the natural sufferings that follow. I will argue and then try to convince others, through compassion, that my suffering is not caused by my disordered choices and acts. Rather, I hold my suffering to be caused by the very claim that any human acts, as such, are immoral. My "suffering," in my view, is caused by the existence of moral standards as such.

Compassion begins with feeling the sufferings of another. It can lead step by step to the overturning of the natural order. It does this by making the suffering I "feel" to be the determinate factor, not the act from which the suffering follows. Aristotle was right. He teaches us that our passions, feelings, or emotions need first to be ruled by our reason before they can support us in living well. Indeed, much of our moral life consists in ruling our passions, which are good in themselves but must be ruled by our reason to a proper end. Compassion has a place in a well-ordered soul. But it cannot, by itself, tell us what this order of soul is. When unsupported by reason, compassion alone can substitute emotion for truth and knowledge of right order.

Chapter 8

On Punishment

Lo, the Lord shall come in fire, his chariots like the whirlwind, to wreak wrath with burning heat and his punishment with fiery flames.

Isaiah 66:15

THOUGH MOST modern men are leery of associating punishment with God, Scripture itself has no such hesitation. When God is said to be "angry," it is always over something that anyone ought to be angry about. Anger itself is a proper emotion and response to obvious evil and injustice. To look upon evil deeds as if they made no difference in the world is to misunderstand either the world or evil. If we had a world in which punishment was neither helpful nor necessary, we would already be in a sinless world, which, quite evidently, we are not.

Where, we might ask, are we to fit an understanding of punishment into our thinking? In a basic sense, it is one of those things, like death, that ought not to be, was never intended to be. Punishment arose because of an event that relates to our freedom. Once the power of choice was first used in a way contrary to our own good and God's purpose for us, punishment came into the picture as a consequence. When a lion kills and eats a zebra, the zebra is not being "punished" for something. Punishment presupposes genuine freedom. We can look on punishment in purely negative terms, as simply mindless and unbridled retribution. But punishment properly speaking is a response to something that was wrongly put into the world by our free choices.

If we list the things for which we are punished, sort them out according to their severity, we obtain a pretty good idea of what the law or the one who carries out the punishing thinks is right and what is wrong. Punishment is conceived as a response to an action that is wrong or evil, to a rule that is violated. The gravity of the punishment is more or less supposed to relate to the seriousness of the fault. We do not punish automobile parking violations the same way that we punish murder. Still, punishments are meted out in response to both. The punishment does not itself establish the reason for thinking some action is wrong and hence susceptible to punishment. Rather punishment is designed to reinforce reason, especially when it is lacking in the one who commits the fault or sin.

This is why "fear of the Lord" can be a good thing. We may at times do the right thing not because we understand it, but because we "fear" the punishment. This "fear," at least, prevents us from doing something irrevocably wrong. If we "intend" to do something wrong, but do not do it because of fear, we still sin, but we leave objective reality as it is. The man we "might have" murdered is still alive and well.

To have a complete understanding of forgiveness and mercy, then, we need to examine punishment. To begin with, two issues must be distinguished. The first is whether some or other act is wrong. Once this issue is decided, punishment is prescribed to show the seriousness of the evil involved. Secondly, just what is a proper punishment is something pertaining to positive law. It can vary by time and circumstance. Prudence will also be needed to determine whether the same punishment is due to every culprit. Many mitigating circumstances can intervene about which it is impossible to legislate in advance.

Yet, we might still ask: "Why punish at all?" I have previously mentioned Plato in regard to the issue of punishment. There is a reason for this. One of the most famous, if not the most famous, discussions of punishment is found in Plato's dialogue *Gorgias*. It is here that Socrates says, much to the horror of a leading politician, that, if we do something wrong, we should not only be punished but, as the *Gorgias* taught, we should *want* to be punished. It is one thing to maintain that a crime ought to be punished, another to argue that the one committing the crime ought to *want* to be punished.

However this view might initially sound, when we look at it carefully, it makes sense. How did Socrates think about this matter of wanting to be punished for our crimes and sins? The first step is that some actual person willingly does some evil act. He almost always does so with some justification in his own mind for doing it. That is, he has an explanation of reality that allows him to do the act. Logically, as we have seen, this reasoning is but another form of pride, now appearing in one's actions.

The deed is next put into the world by choice. The act has its own consequences on the agent and on others. If, say, we kill someone, he is dead. If we rob someone, he is deprived of his rightful goods. The person who does the act is now forever the person who did this or that at a definite time and place. In other words, the world now has within it a lack of a good that ought to have been there. A disorder comes into being that ought not to have existed.

If the man who commits the crime does not change his mind until he dies, he dies with this act on his soul. He will be judged accordingly if Plato and Scripture are right about the Last Judgment. But let us suppose the man realizes that he ought not to have done what he did. In other words, he admits to himself and the world that his action caused disorder in the world, in his life and in that of others. The first thing he needs to do is to acknowledge that he was wrong in doing the act. This is part of what humility means. Next he needs to find a way to rid himself of the responsibility or guilt caused by his sins. He must look about for some means of forgiveness. He realizes that something greater than himself is involved.

The confession of sins in the Sacrament of Penance is the central locus of this forgiveness. It makes us aware of the divine dimensions of all our actions. But the Sacrament's validity depends on the sinner's desire to be forgiven, another free act. To do this, he needs to acknowledge that his effort to rewrite the rules of good and evil was ill-founded. Sins do cause disorder. So now we see that he announces to himself and God at least, but implicitly to everyone, that the law or rule of reason was right all along. He wishes to reaffirm this as a step in repairing the damage of his act. He may not consciously understand every one of these steps, but implicitly this is what he is doing.

The final step is punishment. Socrates had said that the sinner should want to be punished. The worst thing that could happen to him would be not to be punished. Why? Because that would indicate that he really did not admit his action or see its disorder. But when he voluntarily accepts the punishment, he shows to the world that he both understands what the right order is and that he seems, by the sign of this punishment, to restore it and show its seriousness. So punishment is not so irrational after all. If, however, we are just punished with no conscious repentance, confession, or concern about forgiveness, nothing is changed. We are, in principle, still in our sin.

It is often said that the primary purpose of punishment is

either the reform of the criminal or the protection of the public order. Punishment does imply a willingness to repair the evil our acts have caused. It is on this basis that clemency and forgiveness can more easily be offered. But the main point that I want to make in this chapter is that suffering due punishment, willingly, both restores confidence in the goodness of the law of reason and allows us to grant that the one who broke the law now understands its rightness. Punishment in this sense is "suffered." It is not hostile to forgiveness but helps to provide its foundation.

Chapter 9

On Forgiveness

Finally, even if brothers die for brothers, yet no martyr by shedding his blood brings forgiveness for the sins of his brothers, as Christ brought forgiveness to us. In this he gave us not an example to imitate, but a reason for rejoicing.

St. Augustine, On John, 84

WE CANNOT BE "forgiven" for something that we did not do, for something that could not properly be attributed to us. The third and seventh books of Aristotle's *Ethics* are devoted to the question of why we can attribute some action to a given person as its immediate cause. If an action was caused by ignorance, force, or passion it probably could not, properly speaking, be an act of a responsible person, or at least not wholly. On the other hand, if we knew what we were doing and did it, then the action is seen to be ours. We caused it, no one else. All of our actions are done under the aegis of the good, even those that are bad. What we do when we sin is refuse to see the whole context of an issue. We shift our attention away from the reason why the action is wrong to that part of it that is good.

Let us suppose that we do recognize that we are responsible for some deed that is really wrong. We acknowledge it as wrong, as we saw in the previous chapter. We are even punished for it. What we want to look at here is the grounds for not holding us responsible for our acts.

In a homily at Santa Marta (January 23, 2015), Pope Francis spoke of "forgiveness": "God always forgives! He never tires of forgiving. It is we who tire of asking for forgiveness." The Pope recalled the "how many times?" question of Scripture—the "seventy times seven." He did not mention the sin against the Holy Spirit that would not be forgiven. That sin is usually interpreted to mean that the sinner who chooses himself cannot be budged from attention to himself to look at something else. In such cases, the sin cannot be forgiven because it will not be admitted.

Before forgiveness, the sin must be acknowledged. This acknowledgment is what the priest has to hear and judge in confession. Usually, the promise to "sin no more" is presumed. If I confess my sins but do not plan to change my ways, it is difficult to see what forgiveness might mean. Thus, Francis adds: "If you have lived a life of many sins, many bad things, but at the end contritely ask for forgiveness, He forgives you, straight away. . . . We need only to repent and ask for forgiveness."

That God the Father sent His only Son into the world so that sins might be forgiven is at the heart of Christianity. Presumably, everyone knows from his experience that something is wrong in his human condition, something no one has ever quite defined or fully eradicated. Some like to think that the cause of this recurrent historical disorder is the very idea that a man can do something wrong or evil. All we need do to be perfect is rid ourselves of the silly claim that good and evil exist.

Yet, sin seems connected with our very condition. Christianity is not new because men suddenly realized that they sinned. This sense of something disordered existed long before the advent of Christianity. Rather they did not know what to do about the evils that they sent into the world because of their sins. Evidently, not any way would do. The forgiveness had to be placed in the hands of someone authorized to forgive. No ordinary person possessed this capacity.

Of the billions of people who have lived on this planet, few have heard of this forgiveness of sins that revelation postulates. Among those who have heard of it, not many practice it. To cover this situation of revelation not being widely known, many talk of at least being sorrowful. God will forgive, it is argued, even if we know nothing of the context of the sacrament pertaining to forgiveness of sin. Some would extrapolate this claim to assert that all are saved. Others would suspect that, if everyone is forgiven, no matter what they do, why bother being good? If the good and evil are equally redeemed whether the sacrament exists or not, we have no need of a revelation that includes repentance.

On June 3, 1781, Boswell talked to Samuel Johnson about original sin in "consequence of the fall of man, and the atonement made by our Savior." Johnson asked Boswell to record these further reflections: "With respect to original sin, the inquiry is not necessary; for whatever is the nature of human corruption, men are evidently and confessedly so corrupt, that all the laws of heaven and earth are insufficient to restrain them from crimes." Whether we agree with this view or not, Johnson adds that all mankind have recognized the problem and sought means to atone for sin by some sort of sacrifice. "The great sacrifice for the sins of mankind was offered by the death of the Messiah, who is called in Scripture: 'The Lamb of God who taketh away the sins of the world,' Johnson continues. "To judge of the reasonableness of the scheme of redemption, it must be considered as necessary to the governance of the universe, that God should make known his perpetual and irreconcilable detestation of moral evil." One is hard-pressed to find anything more insightfully stated on what is at stake in the reality of forgiveness.

Of particular interest in this passage from Johnson is not the emphasis on God's forgiveness but on the causes in the world itself, the existence and detestation of moral evil. Put briefly, something needs forgiveness. Moreover, no humanly concocted rite or absolution is sufficient to accomplish this atonement. If our sins are forgiven by the Father, whatever they are, it is not because of any remarkable gesture on our part. It begins with a real sacrifice, a real "savior."

God might well have left us in our sins. That He did not does not minimize their heinousness, but emphasizes it. We live in a world that does not choose to admit that anyone sins, a world that claims evils can be eradicated by technical, economic, or psychological means. The sticking point of the Father's forgiveness is not on the side of God, but on our side. The one sin that cannot be forgiven is the one we insist on committing, the sin that says that we need not acknowledge moral evil in our souls or in the encouragement that they receive from our culture.

Chapter 10

On Mercy

Mercy is not of this world, nor compatible with the world's sense of justice, which interprets the former as tolerance and neglect, the latter as ruthless decisions. Yet, in the view of Heaven, they are one and the same; not justice tempered by mercy, but the two infused.

David Warren, "St. Luke's Passion,"
(*The Catholic Thing*, April 1, 2015)

Praised be God, the Father of our Lord Jesus Christ, the Father of mercies, and the God of all consolation!

2 Corinthians 1:3

GOD WOULD BE GOD even if there were no place for mercy in the world. Indeed, God would be God if there were no world at all. In the beginning was God. Nothing existed. Nothing was nothing. God was "*I am.*" We might then ask: "Why does mercy have a place in our world?" St. Paul told the Corinthians that the Father of Jesus Christ is the "Father of mercies." And, in that small phrase, we can see why we would not know of "mercy" unless we needed to know about it. That is, had there been no Fall, no sin, we would only know God as the dispenser of good. There would be no occasion for us to see His mercy. We know about it because we know the reason why Christ was sent into the world in the way He was sent. By His passion and death, He was to provide us with a way for our sins to be forgiven. He did not "need" to do this. He chose to do it. And not just any way would do. Redemption through the Cross was chosen by God as the way to deal with a sinful mankind. If there were no sinners in the actual world *that is*, mercy would not have concerned us. David Warren was right in pointing out that God's justice, love, and mercy are basically together as a whole in His very being. Mercy only arises when something goes wrong. And the only things that can go wrong are rational beings that are free to accept or reject the reason for their creation—which reason is to receive "eternal life"; to participate in their own measure in the inner life of God as their final end.

Perhaps we can come at an understanding of mercy from another angle, one that sees it not merely as a response to chosen injustice. Thomas Aquinas asked himself: "Was the world created in 'justice'?" Surprisingly, perhaps, he did not think so. Why? If the world were created in justice, it would logically mean that the basic principle of justice would have to be operative in this creation. That basic principle, as we saw earlier, was that of rendering what was "due." But to whom could God have owed anything? The origin of the cosmos was thus not out of God's justice.

The very idea of creation being a matter of justice implies a deficiency in God; namely, that somehow He "owed" something to someone not Himself. But the plan of God in the cosmos need not have occurred. The origin of the cosmos and of our place within it lies in the abundance of God's love. It was not, in itself, a response to anything outside of Himself. God's love is creative. He has first loved us. God's own being is love. This is why God is primarily understood as love, not mercy. Thus, the primary character of the world and of us in it is best conceived after the manner of a gift. It is not something "owed," but something given that need not have been given.

St. Thomas concludes that the world is created in mercy and

not justice. By this affirmation, he emphasizes this gratuitous nature of God. When it comes to our actual situation as a fallen race, we see that Christ revealed Himself under the aspects of both justice and mercy. This is why repentance and the Last Judgment remain present in Christ's teaching. Justice does not disappear when God is also seen as merciful. God's love manifests itself as mercy when something deserving of punishment appears in the lives of free creatures.

Aquinas affirmed that the world was not created because God owed something. Thus, if the world does exist, it does so under the aegis of the abundance of love. Included in this love is mercy, which comes into play when acts of injustice take place. Once sin happens, it needs to be acknowledged and perhaps punished. If possible, order needs to be restored and the cause of disorder acknowledged. John Paul II, in reflecting on Divine Mercy Sunday, remarked that God would forgive all that can be forgiven. We see this same idea in Scripture. Christ is asked: "How many times is one's brother to be forgiven?" He responds, "seventy times seven times"; that is, if forgiveness is sought with repentance, then it is given without limit, as Pope Francis also reminds us.

The difficulty, though, is that God cannot just up and wipe the slate clean. He cannot forgive everyone with no participation on the sinner's part. When we sin, we do not just sin against our neighbor or ourselves. A divine dimension also exists in every sin. That dimension can best be described when we understand that God, from the beginning, loves His creation, the persons He creates. The only way for this transcendent dimension of sin to be forgiven would be for a divine response to sin to occur. That appearance of a way to forgive sin is substantially what redemption is about. Christ died to save all men. Their sins are forgiven from God's side.

But every sin has a second aspect. God can forgive, forget, or overlook the transcendent implications of sin, but He cannot impose forgiveness on us. As we have seen, we remain free to accept or to reject the precise manner in which God chose to redeem us, to forgive our sins. Forgiveness requires that we acknowledge our sins. We usually refuse to do this on the familiar grounds that we make our own rules. God's response to our sins was the life of Christ. God could not force us to repent. But He could show us the consequences of our sins as they affected Him in the person of the Word made flesh.

The passion of Christ is the visible manifestation among us of the consequences of sin. But as we say in the Creed, we also "believe in the forgiveness of sins." This is the divine mercy. This means that once we do sin, life goes on with the consequences of the deed or words we have put into existence in our sinning, and what we need to do is to repent of our sins. We do this primarily by stating—with contrition—in the Sacrament what it is we have done wrong. This act restores the order we broke by our action. And we need to be forgiven. We cannot do this for ourselves. We can be sorry. We can know why what we did was wrong. But since our sins have a transcendent dimension, it is God who also must forgive us. Christ came into the world primarily to open this possibility to us.

Where does mercy fit into this picture? First we must realize that what we do that is wrong is no light thing. Each of us is an immortal being. We are warned about hurting or scandalizing even the least of our brethren. God is not concerned with punishing us but with forgiving us. Consequences do follow if we do not have our sins forgiven. Hell simply means that God leaves us with our choices. He must do this. Otherwise, we could not be related to Him as a result of our own choice in the light of His first love of us.

In his encyclical on mercy, John Paul II put it this way: "Properly understood, justice constitutes...the goal of forgiveness. In no passage of the Gospel message does forgiveness, or mercy as its source, mean indulgence towards evil, towards scandal, towards injury or insult" (*Dives in Misericordia*, 14). This is the same point that we made earlier about compassion, how by emphasizing feeling rather than principle, compassion, like mercy, can end in undermining the whole moral order.

Mercy is the divine love that manifests itself when men sin. It is the same love that created them in the first place. They were given abundant life. But God gave them this life in order, as it says in John's Gospel, that we be His friends. Friendship is mutual or else it does not exist at all. Friendship is always a reciprocity, and it does not mean anything if it is not free on both sides. This is the risk of God in creating us: that we would choose not to return the love in which we were created. But even if we refuse, on God's part we can be forgiven. The only thing that remains to us is our free willingness to return God's love by our manifesting it in our own lives. We do this, in part, by acknowledging our sins and asking for forgiveness. From this point on, we no longer fear. We are in the hands of the divine mercy.

Chapter 11

On Moral Reasoning

Of some such kind are the difficulties that arise; some of these points must be refuted and the others left in possession of the field; for the solution to the difficulty is the discovery of the truth.

Aristotle, *Ethics*, 1146b5–6

FORGIVENESS, as we have seen, requires that there is something that needs to be forgiven. It implies that what is forgiven has a cause in us. This cause could only be attributed to us if we were the ones who made it happen in the first place. Explicitly or implicitly, we must have reasoned about the actions that we put out there into existence. We often want to suggest that even if we were involved in an action, we did it because of passion, ignorance, or force. In other words, we often try to show that we were not really responsible. Therefore, we cannot be found guilty. Moral reasoning, unlike theoretical reasoning, involves how we judge a particular action that comes forth from our putting it into effect.

At a nephew's home recently, I looked through his shelves for something to read. I came across a handsome edition of *Huckleberry Finn*. I had not read this book in ages, so I began to look at it again. It is pretty hard to put down. Early in the book, the Widow Douglas reads to Huck about Moses and the Bulrushes. My grandniece wants to know what a "bulrush" is. I tell her.

Huck says: "I was in a sweat to find out all about him." The widow informs him that Moses "has been dead a considerable long time; so then I didn't care no more about him, because I don't take no stock in dead people." Confronted with such a passage, what can a body do but read on?

What got me to thinking was a scene when Jim and Huck are on the raft just about the time they run into the wreck of the steamboat *Walter Scott*. They are still above Cairo, where the Ohio comes in, fixing to go ashore there in a free state and free Jim, or so they thought. Jim was a slave of Miss Watson, a good-enough lady but she needed money and so thought to sell Jim, who was worth $800 in New Orleans. Jim was trying to escape this fate. This was how he and Huck would eventually join forces on Jackson's Island. Huck also was escaping from his boozing Pap, from the Widow Douglas, and from the searchers for his own body. They believed he was floating somewhere in the Mississippi, after he fooled them and Pap into thinking he was drowned, his means to escape.

In order to eat, Jim and Huck slip into a field to "borrow" some needed provisions, or maybe even a chicken. If they happened by a chicken that wasn't "roosting comfortable," they "lifted" it. Huck recalled the shrewd advice of his Pap. "Take a chicken when you get a chance." If you don't want to eat him, you can find someone that does. It creates good will. "A good deed ain't ever forgot." Huck adds, however, that he "never see Pap when he didn't want the chicken himself."

Before daylight, Jim or Huck would canoe ashore, creep into a field to find a watermelon, or mushmelon, or a pumpkin, or new corn. Was this filching all right? Was it moral? Well, "Pap said it warn't no harm to borrow things if you was meaning to pay them back some other time." Intention was everything. Clearly, borrowing "ain't" taking what's not yours. On the other hand, "the widow said it warn't anything but a soft name for stealing and no decent body would do it." Authorities conflicted.

Jim and Huck began to debate this fine ethical point. For his part, Jim split the difference. Pap was "partly" right, he thought, but so was the widow. The solution, Jim offered, was this: they would pick out two or three things from the list of their daily needs. They would then promise not to take them anymore. This seemed like a mighty fine idea. If they did not take anything that they promised not to take, it would be all right to "borrow" the other things. They reckoned that it was no harm to "borrow" the other stuff which they "intended" to return.

This highly refined bit of scholastic casuistry next presented them with the even-more slippery problem of what to put on the list of things they would not "borrow" or intend to "borrow" any more. Drifting down the river, they talked all night to decide what things not to "borrow" anymore.

They did not know whether to drop "the watermelons, or the cantelopes, or the mushmelons, or what." But they had to decide. Near daylight, they resolved their moral dilemma with one of the finest bits of ethical reasoning I have ever seen. In a stroke of genius, Jim and Huck decided to drop "crabapples and p'simmons." It is amazing how much better a fellow feels when he knows that he has resolved a difficult moral problem that has been bothering his soul for some time. "We warn't feeling right before that." Every man has a conscience, even drifting on the Mississippi. "But it was all comfortable now." Huck could relax. "I was glad the way it come out, too." The results of a noble decision are not always so propitious as this one was. "Why was that?" Well, it was "because crabapples ain't ever good, and the p'simmons wouldn't be ripe for two or three months yet." This is clearly "moral reasoning" at its best. It is the best possible solution in the best possible world to one of the world's great ethical dilemmas. We take "no stock in dead people" and never touch "crabapples or unripe p'simmons."

Chapter 12

On "Severe Penances"

These things kindle my wrath, a fire that burns all the day. Lo, before me it stands written; I will not be quiet until I have paid in full your crimes and the crimes of your fathers as well, says the Lord.

Isaiah 65:5–7

IN THE COMPLEX of ideas and words that surround notions of forgiveness and compassion is the word *penance*. Monastic tradition talks of voluntary penance that a saint can impose on himself in reparation for his own or other people's sins. In the Church, the Sacrament of Penance, or confession, is not complete until a suitable "penance" has been imposed on and completed by the penitent. Penance in this sense implies an effort to make the sinner aware that his or her sins actually did disrupt their lives or the lives of others. In the early Church, sometimes we hear of "public," often "severe," penances designed to let a community know that a sinful deed has been confessed and forgiven.

Benedict XVI (General Audience, October 17, 2012) said that many problems are caused by incomplete or inaccurate understandings of the precise words and meanings of doctrine, particularly the Creed. We think that, with a good heart and a rosy outlook, we need not be too exacting about *what* is taught.

Aren't we to obey a "Person," not abstract truths? This is right, provided that we realize that truth exists in a person carefully affirming what is true or denying what is not.

Accuracy of speech and definition stands at the basis of our liberty in law. As Peter Kreeft shows in his *Philosophy of Jesus*, Christ is a precise thinker and speaker. Understanding the "Word made flesh" bears with it a long history of fuzzy thinking that has caused many untoward practical results among us. To say "Christ, the person, is the Truth" does not excuse us from speaking accurately about who and what He is. Not every word means the same thing. We must be sure we use words in the same way.

Frank Sheed, the Australian writer and founder with his wife, Maisie Ward, of the once-famous Catholic publishing house Sheed & Ward, loved to recount his experiences with the Catholic Truth Society. He and his friends would present and debate the particulars of the faith with anyone who appeared at Hyde Park Corner or other famous London debating spots. The rules of the game were to match wits and truth. Recently, I found a Sheed essay entitled "The Church and I" in the January 1975 *Catholic Digest*. Here he recalled these experiences in street-side controversy. Evidently, one day, a colleague of Sheed's was heckled and challenged by a rather raucous and not-too-attractive lady. She had a reputation for expressing her rather negative views of the Church's practices. The CTS man talked of Confession; the lady mockingly interrupted him: "Oh I know you Catholics. Your young men go to Confession in the church across the street from my house. Immediately afterwards, they come over and make love to me." Obviously, this sally needed to be handled gingerly. The CTS man let the import of the lady's accusation hang in the air. Then he very properly replied: "Madam, I had no idea that priests were handing out such *severe penances* these days." Something positive must always be said, I think, for the place of wit in theology!

One has to know enough about Catholic practice and teaching to appreciate the humor of this retort. Many people, themselves *not* believers in sin, still accuse Catholics of hypocrisy because some of them confess their sins, do the penance, and go out, in spite of the admonition, to sin again. Christ Himself was asked how many times we should forgive the sinner. "Up until seventy times seven," he said (Matthew 18:22). The Lord seems to have been less surprised at repeat sinners than we are. He understood, with Aristotle, the difficulty we have in overcoming our vices.

Christ said repeatedly that the righteous have no need for repentance. He came to save sinners, the existence of whom seemed obvious enough. The saving of sinners would logically presuppose a) that sin existed (or, perhaps better, that we failed to do what is good and right when we could) and b) that some means existed whereby such sins could be acknowledged and forgiven. A "penance" was to follow the self-recognition by the sinner that what he did was his fault. Moreover, a sin is not just a disordered human rejection of an objective standard of the good; all sins are personal. They touch the very being of the sinner. This realization explained why men or angels could not "forgive" sins, but only God.

The disorder of sin is something that reaches even to the divinity. Jesus scandalized the Scribes and Pharisees by claiming the power to forgive sins. They well knew that He was claiming a divine power, which He implicitly proved by His miraculous actions following His claim.

In point of fact, "severe penances" were intended to show one's own understanding of the disorder caused by one's own sins. They were the best we could do to restore the damage to the moral order that we caused. Plato rightly had already said that we should will to be punished for this very reason.

The absence of penance, severe or otherwise, I suspect, would signify a world in which nothing we do makes any real difference. Such a world is exactly the opposite of the one God created. In this latter world, two things, wit and sin, can exist side by side. For when the Word was made flesh, sin did not have the final word. This is, no doubt, why we read that more joy is found in heaven over one who repents than ninety-nine just who do not need "repentance" (Luke 15:7). The modern "difficulty" consists in the increasing difficulty of finding the ninety-nine who have no need of repentance. That is, the need of repentance is much more widespread today than the parable indicated.

Chapter 13

On Fame and Envy

He [Christ] was aware, of course, that it was out of envy that the High Priests handed Him over.

Mark 14:19

But they, when they were departed, spread abroad His fame in all that country.

Matthew 9:31

CHRIST WAS HANDED over because of envy. His fame also was a cause of trouble for Him. Had he simply remained out of the limelight, even in the backward place in which He was born, not much notice would have been accorded to Him. But envy can be a terrible thing. It can happen in the lives of the poor and weak as well as the rich and famous. But it manifests itself as a judgment on us. Someone else, we think, is doing what only we should be doing or are worthy to do. Fame given to the wrong person creates a following for him. Often Christ's immediate enemies did not act against Him because they feared the people, who thought him a prophet. Yet fame is a worthy thing. We should honor what is to be honored. Fame is the spiritual reward and recognition of someone else's accomplishment.

The other side of doing penance for our sins and seeking forgiveness is the praise we should offer to those who are virtuous, who do good to others. Such reflections bring us to consider the subject of fame and envy more carefully. Aristotle had implied that envy is a more dangerous vice than greed, even though greed was in general probably more prevalent. Envy is a personal vice of a very spiritual nature. It means refusing to give credit where it is due. Fame, on the other hand, usually involves acknowledging something exceptional, a deed or a word that calls attention to something well or nobly done.

In the literature that concerns clerics and academics we run into a sin called, in Latin, *invidia clericorum*. This vice refers to the envy, *invidia*, manifested by clerics, both lay and religious, over the true accomplishments of others, especially spiritual accomplishments. It is a subtle, dangerous vice. Except for pride, which is not really concerned with what others think, envy is the most dangerous vice, not greed or misuse of pleasure, as we often think. Why? Indeed, in Christianity, while envy is very dangerous, the most dangerous vice is pride, *superbia*. In its essence, pride means using our admitted freedom to make ourselves, not God, the center of reality. Pride means to make ourselves the cause of the distinction of good and evil so that what is evil or what is good depends on our own definition of it. This places us at the center of things.

Envy and vanity are two more-or-less related vices. Envy is certainly more dangerous than vanity, though not so perilous as pride. Both envy and vanity are concerned with others; pride is only concerned with the self. Chesterton once remarked that vanity is a rather "healthy" vice. It is located, unlike pride, outside of ourselves. Vanity is concern about how we look to others. How we look to others is not under our control. Yet, to wonder how we look to others is not wrong. Vanity is a mild vice because it tends to prefer how we look to others to whether we are truly good. If we are good but do not seem so to others, it should not matter. But it is not a vice to strive to look well to others.

Envy refers to our giving or withholding honor to others to whom it is due. To be the object of fame means that we not only look good to others, but that our abilities or looks or accomplishments are indeed acknowledged by them. Fame has the connotation of great notoriety; to attain fame need not be a vice unless it is sought for its own sake apart from some objective accomplishment. Envy, however, always has the element of something disordered, something distorted. Envy means that we withhold honor that is due.

Envy is thus a more spiritual thing than, say, greed, which is concerned with material possessions. Envy deals with spiritual goods. It is sometimes difficult to understand that things that are worthy of honor should be honored. Honor means that some human being positively acknowledges something good in what another has done or what he is. To "honor" thy father and mother thus does not mean to give them material goods. It means to acknowledge in an appropriate way what they are and have done. Aristotle pointed out that honor may be proposed as a possible definition of happiness. Many people locate happiness in honor, which is more political in context, more concerned with how others see us. Politicians are often tempted by honor rather than by riches or pleasures. But the reason that honor cannot be the definition of happiness is that it does not depend on us. It depends on the free acknowledgment of others of whatever talents or accomplishments we might have.

How does envy work? We know it is one of the capital sins. That is, it is a source of other sins. When someone we do not like does something that is truly worthy, we know that we are envious if we are reluctant to congratulate the accomplishment of the other person. If someone is appointed to a job or receives a reward that is truly deserved, we "owe" honor or praise for that accomplishment. The other person cannot "demand" it of us. So it must come out of our free will to recognize something worthy in another.

Thus, envy falls into a world in which human beings are supposed to respond. They are called to acknowledge something worthy in the words or deeds of another. We are not talking here of anything false or phony. We are talking of real accomplishments that ought to be recognized and acknowledged. Envy, unlike greed, is spiritual. It is not concerned with wealth or goods. Envy, in this sense, remains within us, even though it is obvious to others that we do not respond objectively to the works or artistry of another.

I do not wish to identify enjoying fame with envy. The praise of others is no doubt exhilarating, whether it be in a beauty contest, an elevation to the cardinalate or senate, the winning of a game, or election to the board of directors of a major corporation. The principle of justice intimates that something which cannot be repaid exactly in kind, as is impossible in spiritual things, still needs some manifestation. Fame is beyond justice. It is what must be given when financial considerations are already met.

Moreover, the fame of one can occasion the envy of another. It takes a clear eye to see the presence of envy in our souls. But fame is, or ought to be, the way we know what we consider worthy, what we consider right. Fame means that something worthy has been accomplished by one of our kind. No doubt, fame can be notorious. Fame is also given to unworthy things.

Tell me what you praise and I will tell you what you are. Likewise, if you tell me what you envy I will tell you what you are. In either case, we are close to the heart of the spiritual things that motivate us. Both fame and envy point to what is worthy of praise and whether we possess it in ourselves. Aristotle talks of the famous magnanimous man, the man who is noble and knows he is noble. His sense of his own worthiness is not a lie. It acknowledges what he is. We ought to strive to be worthy of proper praise. We are to let our lights shine before men (Luke 8:18). We ought also to strive to keep our eyes and hearts on things worthy of praise. We ought never to separate praise from what is worthy of it.

In the end, we are to praise God, who is most worthy of our praise. That is to say, we ought to recognize what we are. We are not the maker of things. We are created. We are receivers. We are given something worthy in our very being. We see that what is worthy comes from others. Our fame points to a fame that is not ours to have, but only ours to acknowledge. This is why our highest act is of celebration and praise, of acknowledging, not envying, what is not ours but what is given to us by *what is*.

Chapter 14

Screwtape on Pleasure

One day, when the sons of God came to present themselves before the Lord, Satan also came among them. And the Lord said to Satan, "Whence do you come?"

Job 1:6–7

A FORMER STUDENT, now teaching seniors in a public high school, told me that she briefly reads out loud each day. One book she read to her students was, surprisingly, C.S. Lewis's saga of the devil's mind, *The Screwtape Letters*. I knew that I had a copy. Frankly, I had only read parts of it. So I decided to begin reading a daily chapter.

Actually, earlier I recalled Screwtape's advice to Wormwood, a minor devil assigned to keep a young atheist corrupted. Screwtape told him to watch the man's reading. For "the young atheist cannot be too careful of the books he reads." Every time I think of that passage, I laugh. Atheists have to be careful lest their open minds corrupt their closed doctrine. Lewis himself is a dangerous read for an atheist. So is Chesterton. Catholics don't usually have the reverse problem. We like to read the atheists to brush up on our logic by identifying their frequent lack of it.

In the Ninth Letter, Screwtape advises Wormwood as to how a devil ought or ought not to handle pleasure. The classic discussion of pleasure is in Aristotle. Basically, he tells us that every human activity, including thinking, has its own proper pleasure. Pleasure is intrinsic to the act in which it occurs: the pleasure of seeing or smelling. We would want to see or smell even if no distinct pleasure went along with it. The rightness or wrongness of pleasure depends on the rightness or wrongness of the act in which it occurs. The pleasure, as such, is always good, part of the good of creation itself.

Thus, when we do something for the pleasure in the act instead of the intrinsic purpose of the act, its own end, we shift our attention away from what is really going on. In effect, we choose to make pleasure our immediate end, not the act's end in which it occurs. This is as true when we drink beer as if it is not also a food or use contraceptives to "enjoy" the pleasure but ignore the act's own inner purpose.

Just how we manage to do these things is also addressed in Aristotle. Basically, we use our will to select what we want to do. We suppress considering what the act is about, to focus its pleasure. Then we give a thousand "reasons" why it is all right to do so.

With such background in mind, we see how Screwtape explains to Wormwood why even the devils have to be careful with pleasure. It is much trickier than they realize. The devil is initially in the business, not of eradicating pleasure, but of skewering or diminishing it, changing its meaning, isolating it so that, as Aristotle stated, it cannot "blossom" to enhance the normal act for which it is designed.

So Screwtape first advises Wormwood: "Never forget that when we are dealing with any pleasure in its healthy and normal and satisfying form, we are, in a sense, on the Enemy's ground." "The Enemy" in that sentence is God. The "we" are the devils. This is Genesis! Devils can sometimes tell the truth. The fact is—and this bothers them—that normal pleasure is

God-given. This is "mere Christianity," to use Lewis's phrase. The devils know their catechism.

Screwtape admits that the devils manage to win many souls over with the pleasure tactic. Still, "He [God] invented it." By themselves, devils have not managed to produce a single pleasure. What the devils can do—and this is Screwtape's advice—is to encourage us to take those pleasures that "the Enemy [God] has forbidden" (i.e., in the Commandments) in the wrong ways, at the wrong times, or in the wrong degrees.

Thus, the devils "always try to work away from natural conditions of any pleasure, to that in which it is less natural, less redolent of its Maker, and least pleasurable." What an extraordinary sentence! That sentence alone exposes the folly of most of our favorite sins. And, on top of it all, every misuse of pleasure ends up being precisely "less pleasurable." This ironic insight is simply the empirical experience of most people, if they would but admit it.

So what Screwtape concludes, rather philosophically, is this: "An ever-increasing craving for an ever-diminishing pleasure is the formula." The decrease in pleasure is proportion to the deviation of the act from its natural purpose. To accomplish this little deception is, in the devil's view, "better *style*." The word *style* is in italics in Lewis. How amusing! The "style" pages!

The great diabolic ambition is "To get a man's soul and give him nothing in return." Screwtape claims this latter feat "gladdens Our Father's [i.e., Satan's] heart." What a perfect ending! The logic of the improper use of pleasure is, finally, no pleasure at all. This too is the modern world.

Chapter 15
On Losing the Faith

He [Christ] went on to say: "This is why I have told you that no one can come to me unless it is granted him by the Father." From this time on, many of his disciples broke away and would not remain in his company any longer.

John 6:63–64

THE RELATION BETWEEN loss of faith and sins, especially those concerning the sixth commandment in its various forms, is no doubt very close in the modern age. The shadow of the famous aphorism often attributed to the Devil, "*Non serviam*" ("I will not serve"), reflects this defiant refusal. Nothing is to be accepted except in the name of one's own authority. Yet, faith is initially a gift, not something "due" to us. In a way, the rejection of a gift is the most sophisticated insult we can give someone.

Faith is closely related to understanding. Faith seeks understanding, while understanding, not able to grasp everything by itself, leads to faith. The testimony of another is the source of knowledge about the higher things, even of normal things like how we ought best to live to be happy. The Gospel of John itself records instances of disciples who, on hearing what they are to know and believe, depart, unable or unwilling to accept it. Like all those who lose the faith or refuse to accept it, the basic reason is that they think that some way to their happiness can be found other than the "way" that is Christ who leads to the Father (John 14:6).

Estimates vary, but as many as twenty or thirty percent of the American populace was once Catholic. Islam can probably take over Europe and America if its followers just continue reproducing (which they are not doing in some Islamic countries). Europeans and Americans continue their population decline. This leads to the need to find other laborers to replace non-existent children of natives.

We see many conversions to the faith, but also mass defections. Many Evangelical sects have a field day among Latin American Catholics. Christians disappear within many Muslim countries. Many are expelled or killed. From a Christian viewpoint it is a new age of martyrdom. Still, a surprising number of Protestant ministers, for instance, in the spirit of Scott Hahn's *Rome Sweet Home*, enter the Church. Often they realize, as a result of reading Church Fathers on the continuity of Catholicism, that there was no "break" in Christendom from the end of the Apostolic age till the Reformation, as they had been taught there was. The main problem is what to do with these converts in terms of employment. Often they are among the most graphic and effective presenters of the faith.

But the attrition of Catholics from orthodoxy is astonishing. John Paul II and Benedict XVI talked of living in a relativistic and positivist culture. Many of the legislative and judicial decisions that have rejected basic Catholic teachings came from Catholics or were passed with their support. The major facilitators of such decisions claim that they are "Catholic." The bishops rarely say much in particular about this phenomenon that cannot but confuse the public. Presidential candidates and *New York Times* editorials speak of coercing, of eliminating from the public order dissent on abortion or same-sex marriage.

We know people who have "lost the faith." That is a curious expression. Faith is a grace. Though there is reason and good sense to it, we do not simply deduce it from certain premises. It is a gift. But gifts come to us freely. We do not "earn" them. Thus it is easy to undervalue what we have received. Often something that has been given freely is not cherished, which is just the opposite of what a gift is intended to accomplish.

Some people, to be sure, have to study, pray, and work to become Catholics. A gift of faith also needs to be understood. Faith is directed to reason. Reason must rise to receive it. Gifts are easy to lose if we do not appreciate them. Losing the faith is more like throwing a gift away than like losing an argument or a billfold. For the most part, losing the faith, formally or informally, is the result of wanting, choosing to do something that is against the faith.

Once we have decided that we want to do or think something, we have to concoct reasons in defense of our choice. No one can lose or give up Catholicism without a "reason." This giving-up means that we have specifically to reject the reasons why it is not all right to do so. We can only reject these if we propose an alternate "theory" of reality to the position the Church holds.

Socrates proposed that ignorance was the cause of disorder or sin in the soul. No doubt, we find an element of ignorance in any sin or error. But something more is always to be found. Faith is the result primarily of God seeking us. We sometimes fail to realize that our lives are not one-sided affairs. We think we are the only ones doing the seeking, that God just sits there doing His own thing while we rush about. This fact that we are first sought is what the parable of the Lost Sheep is about; it is why we cannot be settled in our aberrations.

Modern notions of freedom are based on the relativist proposition that nothing is true. This position is convenient. It justifies our unwillingness to take anything but ourselves into consideration. If I "feel" like doing this or that, well, it is all right. Of course, no one generalizes this position in such a fashion that what someone else does to us is quite all right. We still have to protect ourselves from someone else's freedom.

The notion that we are the cause of our own good, and so no one else can tell us anything about the important things, has a shadow of a truth, as all error does. We are indeed the architects of what we shall be, of how we present ourselves to God and the world. The primary source of energy in the world is the soul of the individual human person. His life is an arena in which he decides how he, who already exists, will define himself to be. He will define himself in his actions and his thoughts.

The loss of faith is also a choice. It is not just the taking-back of a gift. It is a rejection of it. The rejection may not be in explicit words, though often it is in words that seek to "justify" the loss in terms of another good or idea. In the end, the loss of faith does not mean that God ceases to seek us. It does mean that we cease to seek Him in the manner in which He has guided us, the way of our redemption—that is, the following of Christ.

Chapter 16

On Forgiven and Forgotten Sins

You burdened me with your sins, and wearied me with your crimes. It is I, I, who wipe out, for my own sake, your offenses, your sins I remember no more.

Isaiah 43:24–25

[The Holy Spirit] also says: "Their sins and their transgressions I will remember no more."

Hebrews 10:17

THE FACT OF SINS is one thing. Their forgiveness is another. Judgment and punishment decide the seriousness and consequences of the wrong that is done. Steps are taken to prevent sins and to deal with the one who causes the problem. Christ said that more joy is found in heaven over one sinner who repents than over ninety-nine who have nothing to repent (Luke 15:7). We usually look at sin from the angle of its reality and the need to do something about it. But another fruitful way to think about our lives is to ask: "What becomes of forgiven sins?" Once sins are forgiven, should we brood on them? Certainly we should not become scrupulous and constantly worry that we have not done everything we need to do to explain why we committed them.

In approaching this issue, we must think of it in terms of why evil exists in the world. It exists as a consequence of freedom within a good creation. God's initial response to sin was not to destroy the world or the sinner. Rather it was to let it go on with its consequences. God's response to sin was His mercy. That is, it was that aspect of His original love that manifested itself when things did not go as they should have.

Briefly put, instead of responding by destroying the sinner, God responded by sending His only-begotten Son into the world. As we have noted before, God could not "force" men to repent. That would mean He had made them free and not free at the same time. But He could invite them on their own to repent, especially once the consequences of their sins became manifest to them.

In a famous passage that St. Thomas cites from St. Augustine (I–II, 90, 1, ad 3), God is said to only permit evil in the world if, by it, a greater good will result. In a paradoxical way, then, we can say that every sin is itself an occasion for some other good to come into the world, one that usually is totally outside the comprehension of the sinner. Moreover, any repentant sinner who realizes the full weight of his deed, needs to understand that it is all right for him to go on living. He cannot forget the fact of his sin. But he is not to commit suicide or to lapse into a complete depression. Once sins are forgiven, they are forgiven. Strictly speaking, God does not bring good out of evil per se. Evil is not a "thing," but the lack of something due. A sin is an act we put into the world that lacks proper order. But sin always has aspects of the good in it. It is out of this good that the redemption of sins can take place.

Christ said to the woman, "Go and sin no more" (John 8:11). God "forgets" our sins in the sense that they no longer are held against us. This does not mean that they never happened. For-given sins are not literally "forgotten," however. They become the source from which their initial damage begins to be repaired. "Lord, be merciful to me, a sinner": in this prayer, a man identifies himself for what he is (Luke 18:13). We need not, indeed ought not, pester everyone by telling them how bad we were. That could be a kind of pride or boasting. But we do not wish to deny the truth of our lives.

A question we might ask ourselves is this: "Is there any 'good' in forgiven sins?" As we mentioned, we are familiar with the notion of bringing good out of evil, or better of bringing the good out of the good in which evil exists. Such a question about the good of forgiven sins, no doubt, would only arise if we accepted the central teaching of the New Testament about the forgiveness of sins. In our souls, we carry both forgiven and unforgiven sins with us, if that is what they are. The whole issue of contrition and confession is one thing. The priest says finally: "I absolve you from your sins." He does not do this absolving on his own authority but "through the ministry of the Church in the name of the Father, the Son, and the Holy Spirit." He is an instrument, not a cause.

In Plato's discussion of the final judgment in the last book of the *Republic*, he postulates the possibility of our choosing a new life, a new "spirit," after this present disordered one. What we freely did in this life conditions what we chose in the next. The implication is that if we do not live a virtuous life the first time around, it is not likely that we will do much better with a second or third lifetime. This is the same point that is made in the story of Dives and Lazarus in the New Testament (Luke 16:19–31). Basically, this Platonic account is in accord with the New Testament and with Aristotle. It affirms that we have this one life in which what we are for eternity is decided ultimately by ourselves, by how we respond to the call to repentance, by how we choose to live and deal with our own actions.

In thinking of "forgiven sins," it is clear that any deed, good or bad, once done, or any word once spoken, does not change. What could have been otherwise is fixed by our choice. Like all acts once put in effect, they remain what they are forever. But someone who has sinned, repented, confessed, even been punished, speaks with great authority. He knows he had a problem. He thus becomes a witness to the truth of what the Gospel is about. The witness of the sinless Christ was to take on the sins of the world in His suffering.

The witness of the repentant sinner is of great worth to those who need to understand the consequences of their own actions. The sinless sometimes seem to speak with less insight than the repentant sinner. We look at the two thieves crucified next to Christ. Both were punished (as the repentant thief acknowledged) for just reasons. One asked Christ to bring him down from the cross if Jesus was the Messiah. The other simply asked to be remembered when He came into His Kingdom (Luke 24:39–43). It is quite clear that the testimony of the repentant thief was the one that we remember.

Augustine's famous "confessions" are devoted to remembering his sins before God in order to set the record straight. Once Augustine knew that God acknowledged his awareness of his own sins, he could go on. In both Isaiah and its reference in Hebrews that began this chapter, God says that our sins would be no longer "remembered." This passage provides us with some understanding about the divine mercy in the context of the forgiveness of sins. As I have said before, this "not remembering" does not mean that the fact of what we did is forgotten. The consequences of our sins remain realities and forces in the world, even when repented.

This "not remembering" of God means rather that we can be assured that events will take place that God has willed to happen in spite of our sins. Suppose a good woman's husband is murdered. In a few years she remarries and has children who could not have existed unless the first crime had taken place. Whether the one who committed the murder was repentant or not makes a difference, as does the question of whether the husband was ready to die when he did. But what came from something that should not have happened, that is the murder, is God's way of "not remembering" our sins and crimes. In the end, our forgiven sins are forgotten in our repentance. But they exist in the world as facts out of which goods that we do not and cannot anticipate arise. The love of God is shown in the mercy of God. It is the same creative love that brings goods into existence that could not have otherwise come to be.

We only need to add that unrepented sins also have their consequences. Out of them also does God's mercy work good for others. But God cannot and does not force repentance. This is why the question of Plato about whether the world was created in injustice always remains. Ultimately, a time comes when all the good implicit in both repented and unrepented sins are accomplished in God's mercy. What remains, evidently, is an eternity of abiding by our choice, by that same choice, presented first in Genesis, of whether "men will be like gods" who claim themselves to define the distinction of good and evil, rather than receiving it as a gift that alone completes their own lives.

Chapter 17

On Mercy and Mercilessness

IN THE MAGNIFICAT, we read: "He [the Lord] has mercy on those who fear him in every generation." Those who do not "fear" Him evidently do not come off so easily. Why not? It is no accident that mercy is bound up with fear. What is forgiven is still worthy of the punishment that any disorder rightly deserves—whether forgiven or not. Mercy too has a component of intelligence designating what it is. Forgiveness of sin does not mean that what was forgiven was not evil. It means that it was. Mercy only comes into view when something that ought not to be actually occurs in the world through free agency.

The words *mercy* and *love* are not exactly the same. We love all being because, and only because, it is good. Mercy comes into view when something is not good, when evil is present in our souls. But if we do not acknowledge our part in an evil initiative and intend to correct it, mercy cannot gain entrance.

Chesterton said that the opposite of "funny" is not "serious." Its opposite is "not funny." Similarly, the opposite of mercy is not "just" but "merciless." Mercy is directly related to justice, a good. A fully just world, in which everyone has what is "due" to him, has no need of mercy at all, though it does have need of the love that goes to the core of the good in a way that justice does not.

St. Thomas remarks that the world is not created in justice. If it were, that would imply that God "owed" something to someone not Himself. The world's existence is a result of gratuitousness, not justice. The world has no cause in itself to explain why it exists other than the suspicion that good might freely diffuse itself in being.

Mercy is a more surprising and restrictive word than we might at first realize. We want what goes on in the world, of course, to be "just." But if it is only just, which it isn't, then all actual crimes and sins that occur within it must be requited according to the degree of their disorder. Unpunished sins are very unsettling. They make the world itself seem unjust, as Plato correctly saw. This is, indeed, why he proposed a "last judgment."

Mercy is the forgiveness of what need not or even ought not be forgiven. Indeed, mercy follows after, not before, both forgiveness and punishment. Mercy was never designed to minimize the heinousness of sins or to eliminate their possibility. It was meant to affirm their disorder. But their disorder does not prevent God from "forgetting" them to allow us to begin anew. Thus, God does not just "forgive" sins because He is merciful. He forgives them in the context of our realizing and acknowledging their disorder. Mercy is designed to encourage virtue, not to undermine it.

Pope John Paul II said rightly that God would forgive everything that could be forgiven. Evidently, some things even God cannot do. He cannot forgive one who does not freely ask to be forgiven. If He could or would forgive everyone whether repented or not, it would mean that we could wander about with terrible sins on our souls that were simply ignored. When God said that our sins would be "blotted out," He meant those things which we identify as sins when we acknowledge that we committed them and recognize that we ought not to have done so. These are the sins wherein mercy becomes relevant.

Mercy, paradoxically, can, if we are careless, become merciless. How so? Suppose an all-merciful God forgives all sins, whether repented or not. Everybody thus saves his soul automatically. We do not have to worry about what we do. The "merciful" God has already taken care of us whatever we do. Notice: no input on our part is required. God's merciful love is said to be unrestricted. It is not limited by the distinction of good and evil.

But if everything is forgiven with no indication on our part that we acknowledge what is wrong and intend to cease doing it, this awareness empowers the merciless to do whatever they want. They too are already forgiven. This misunderstanding of mercy would create a jungle.

The second Jesuit Superior General, Diego Laynez, said that "The throne of justice must not be turned into the throne of mercy. To do so is prejudicial to grace. It results in the denial of purgatory." Benedict XVI made the same point in *Spe Salvi*. He pointed out that purgatory makes a good deal of sense when we realize the heinousness of our sins and our need to repent of them even if forgiven. If the forgiveness of sins is automatic with mercy, we have no need of fear or grace to help us to realize and acknowledge our own disorders that alone are the objects of mercy.

Chapter 18

On Necessarily Making Us "Good"

There is no such entity in nature as "evil"; "evil" is merely a name for the privation of good. There is a scale of value stretching from earthly to heavenly realities, from the visible to the invisible; and the inequality between these goods makes possible the existence of them all.

Augustine, *City of God*, XI, 22

There is something in Plato's morality which does not really belong to Plato but is only to be met with in his philosophy, one might say, in spite of Plato: namely, Socratism, for which he was really too noble. "No one wants to do injury to himself, therefore all badness is involuntary. For the bad man does injury to himself: this he would not do if he knew that badness is bad. Thus the bad man is bad only in consequence of an error; if one cures him of his error, one *necessarily makes him— 'good.'*"

Nietzsche, *Beyond Good and Evil*, 190

WE ALWAYS MUST consider forgiveness and repentance in the context of the fact of something that needs forgiveness or repentance. We thus always arrive back at the issue of evil, of whether it is the result of choice or necessity. The first sentence of Julia Wedgwood's 1894 book *The Moral Ideal* reads: "*No deeper cleft* divides human spirits than that which separates the faith possible to men for whom Evil means a mere negation, a mere shadow, a form of ignorance, from that which regards it as an actual existence, a real antagonism to good." This sentence contains both Socrates—"a form of ignorance"—and Satan—"a real antagonism to good." Wedgwood is concerned with what "divides" precisely "human spirits." It has something to do with the way they understand Evil. One will evidently live very differently if he logically follows out the implications of one or the other thesis.

In a real sense, the "bad man" does injure himself. Cicero's natural law also teaches this ironic effect: that our own chosen Evil ultimately harms us. There is validity to the point. But, as Nietzsche also said against Socrates, the cure of "badness" is not simply to "know" what is good. Aristotle insisted that we can only become good by doing good things. He granted that we also must know what things are good. That "All badness is involuntary" is, as Nietzsche hinted, false. All true "badness," on the contrary, is voluntary. As such, as we have seen, a free being can look back on his free actions and freely seek to repair their damage or freely refuse to do so.

An "intelligence" component to badness or evil nonetheless is present in actions that are designated as properly "evil." This intelligence indicates the "direction" an action, in which some good is lacking, will take. This same intelligence will also indicate how it is that "good" can come of "evil." It does not come from the "evil" as such. It comes from the good of the being in which evil is "present" as a lack of what ought to be there.

To lose a limb to disease or an accident is an "evil," but not, as such, a moral one. To put into existence an act of intemperance, injustice, or imprudence is a moral evil. It exists without what it should have in its wholeness. This lack is not a mere "negation." It is due to the actor who puts, and knows that he puts, into reality an act that lacks what is due to it.

As the title of Julia Wedgwood's book suggests, moral "evil" has her attention. Her concern is not with what is known as "metaphysical" evil, that is, with "evil" that does not have connected with it an element of human, or even angelic, choice. It is this "choice" that is the root of all praise or blame for our deeds. This praise or blame indicates our awareness of the moral dimension of each human act without which it is not completely understood. Does evil mean, then, that we are caught up in a dramatic cosmic conflict that really has nothing to do with ourselves? Or are we also involved in its very coming to be? Are our choices involved in what is good or bad, in how either comes to exist? Or are we "good" simply if we know what "evil" is? As Nietzsche implied, it seems highly unlikely.

At first sight, one wonders whether Wedgwood's formulation had a touch of Manicheanism about it. That is, does it imply a "god of good" and "a god of evil" as necessary for the explanation of evil among us? Is matter evil and spirit good, as the Manicheans of every age teach us? If so, the essence of sanity is to reject this dichotomy, without at the same time making evil out to be a mere illusion.

The Genesis account of Creation makes all matter precisely "good," against the Manichean thesis that it is evil. But Genesis also implies a spiritual component to evil that is neither ignorance nor an alien power. Wedgwood's initial sentence in the passage quoted above is not clear on this point. Between ignorance and something with a "real antagonism to the good," a third alternative can be proposed. That in-between position posits something that is good but can choose not to be good. This is what human rational freedom means.

But once a choice for good or evil is made, it cannot simply be "undone." A choice to do an evil act can be regretted and acknowledged as an aberration. This is the closest we can come to restoring what is wrong. The whole drama we know as redemption has to do with a clear understanding of the consequences of our acts and a source for a judgment about their ultimate status. It is also the context of forgiveness and the possibility of reversing the direction of evil back to what is good.

The "deep cleft" that divides us is not that between rich and poor, or that between the "races," or between democratic and non-democratic. Nor is it that between the ill and the healthy, the old and the young, spirit and matter, or equal and unequal. It is not between the intelligent and the dull. These divisions are real enough. Their differences, however, are precisely what make a "whole" composed of many diverse kinds of beings possible, as Augustine suggested. Without this possibility, there could be no "world," no common good properly speaking. But these differences of nationality, race, or sex do *not* as such define man's ultimate character, how he stands before reality. He is an actor in his own personal being.

We do not escape the problem of evil by formulating theories about it that do not penetrate to its essence. Burke's famous remark that "Men of letters, fond of distinguishing themselves, are rarely averse to innovation" is a sober reminder that much of the philosophic enterprise is designed to present a picture of reality that does not conform to *what is*. This alternate picture of reality almost always is formulated to explain "evil" in a way in which, as it were, evil is not what evil is.

Men of letters, the "intellectuals," often think that they need not be obedient to the laws of being, to *what is*. They only need to be "intelligent." The resources of their own thought alone are sufficient to explain the world in which they choose to live. Their minds do not conform to *what is* because, at bottom, *what is* contains a differing understanding of evil than they chose to acknowledge. Their "innovations," as Burke called them, are drawn up to enable them to do, not what they ought, but what they want. This is not a vice of intellectuals alone, to be sure. Yet this vice is more dangerous in their hands because of what is first in their heads.

The notion that evil is a "mere negation" is, of course, the classic Platonic-Augustinian idea that evil is the "lack" of a good, though hardly a "mere" negation. A negation, as such, has no "being." All evil resides in a good being, a person. He implicitly decides not to be good in some choices he makes. Evil is thus an induced "negation" or rather a "privation." It remains alive in the good in which its absence exists. It keeps its presence until it is stopped. "How to stop it?" remains the real problem of evil. Its stopping is the point where grace and nature meet. It seems that mankind as such does not have either the will or capacity to stop evil's continuing reign among us.

The classic definition of evil is "The lack of a good in a being where it ought to exist." So, evil is not a "mere" negation. The word "not" is *not* a bad word. It is, in fact, the instrument of thought whereby we affirm or deny this thing or that thing. The principle of contradiction affirms that "This is not that." It allows us to distinguish real things. It prevents us from collapsing all things into one undifferentiated mass. If we do this, we logically deny our own individual existence. Not a few religious and philosophical positions, often out of despair, take this path, a path that ultimately must end by making evil to be part of the good.

What is of further interest about the passage from Wedgwood is that it talks about the "faith possible to men" under these two propositions about evil: a) that it is a mere negation and b) that it has real existence. Wedgwood is aware of the dryness that comes when we make evil a mere negation and not a real "antagonism" to the good. St. Paul said that our struggles are not so much with "flesh and blood" as with "principalities and powers." These latter terms are used to refer to the angelic intellects of fallen angels (Ephesians 6:12). There is personal drama in our struggles with evil.

Everyone today is loath to think on these questions, though movies and novels with diabolic themes still retain their power and popularity. The notion of "temptation" always bears with it the suspicion of a spiritual or personal power moving in to influence us. We are familiar with characters like Iago or Dr. Faust who imply that evil has behind it a personal, extremely cunning intelligence.

While evil is not itself a "thing," it nevertheless has an intelligence component. As I like to put it, it carries things to their logical conclusion. Aristotle, in his *Ethics*, was already aware that a "small error in the beginning leads to a large error in the end." The truth or falsity of our ideas is not an indifferent matter. They lead to existence in one way or another.

It is part of the "goodness" of the human mind that it can and should know the full dimensions of evil among us. Creation itself is of what is good. But, since freedom is also within created reality, the possibility of choices against the good will also be known. To know evil is not necessarily to do it. Yet, what is perhaps the most fascinating of intellectual exercises is to follow out what is likely to happen and what does happen in reality when what is evil is chosen and carried into effect.

Etienne Gilson remarked in *The Unity of Philosophical Experience* that we are perhaps "free" to choose the beginning principles on which we shall act, including the first principles of being. But once we choose them, we are no longer free to think as we will but only as we can. That is, our chosen first principles, if they are not also the first principles of being, will operate to prevent us from taking certain paths lest we are forced to deny the validity of what we initially willed. We willed it so that we could justify our doing whatever we want.

In the beginning of this chapter, I cited a passage from Augustine concerning the fact that evil is the lack of a good that ought to be there. In that passage, he goes on to remark that the inequality of differing beings in the universe is itself a good. That is, it is good that there is not only one kind of being. This position implies that the life of the hind and the life of the lion are both good, but the existence of one means the death of the other. A similar problem arises among free, rational beings. If we were to prevent them from choosing evil, they would not be the kind of beings they are, whose freedom is precisely their autonomy to see and choose what is really good. If it is not chosen, it does not really belong to them after the manner in which they exist, that is, as rational beings.

Augustine's solution is famous. All of this evil is "permitted" so that a greater good might be possible. It sounds plausible enough, provided we are clear about what the greatest good of creation is. But many a philosopher is enraged by such a view. Evil is ever at the crux of our rebellion from the reality *that is*. Augustine called it *superbia*, pride, the notion that we could and would produce a better world by our own "innovations." Indeed, we might say that the whole history of the modern world and its "innovations" has been charged with the burden of producing this better world than the one given. We are left with what we have produced as an alternative. We were allowed our choices. And in more and more cases, what we have produced is the opposite of what is implied in the law of *what is*.

Let me conclude with Nietzsche's remark about "Socratism," the notion that we "necessarily become good" if we know what is evil. He seems to suggest that the "innovations" of men of letters that would explain an alternative to being—the whole drama of the modern world—do not explain the *things that are.* Julia Wedgwood's search for the "deep cleft" that divides human spirits seems a worthy enterprise. Our understanding of evil does divide us.

The solution is not to claim that there is no evil, or that everything is by nature either good or bad. Ultimately the pursuit of being brings us back to how we live. It is this "how we live" that, as Aristotle said, first guides us to seeing the truth. Augustine's "two cities"—the City of God and the City of Man—remain present among us. This is the "cleft" that divides us. It runs not through nations, classes, structures, religions, or races. It runs through how we live as persons according to the free being we are given, not through the "innovations" that we think are better than *what is.* The only thing that cannot be forgiven is the being that chooses not to be forgiven. As Plato understood—and Augustine followed him on this—in the end only two cities exist.

Chapter 19

On a Cross-Less Catholicism

People going by kept insulting Him, tossing their heads and saying: "Ha, Ha! So you were going to destroy the temple and rebuild it in three days! Save yourself now by coming down from the Cross!" The chief priests and scribes also joined in and jeered: "He saved others but He cannot save Himself! Let the Messiah, the king of Israel, come down from the Cross here and now so that we can see it and believe in Him."

Mark 16:29–32

IN A SINLESS WORLD, forgiveness would not be needed. If we did not need forgiveness, we would not need to deal with the sufferings that arise from our evil choices. Already in the New Testament we find the Cross presented as God's way of redeeming us, of indicating to us the seriousness of His intentions for us. The Messiah was told to come down from the Cross; then everyone would believe. If Christ wanted everyone to believe, why did He not just come down? Basically, as Abraham told the rich man in the parable of Dives and Lazarus, because it would not have worked (Luke 16:19–31). In redeeming us, God did not intend to take away the effects of our sins, only their guilt, if we would accept this.

In a piece in *The Australian* (May 22, 2010), Tess Livingston covers the New Missal. Cardinal Pell was instrumental in the English re-translation. This good work needed early explanation. Of the present translation, Cardinal Pell remarks: "The previous translators seemed a bit embarrassed to refer to angels, sacrifice and perpetual virginity. They went softly on sin and redemption."

Though they must be put in a larger context, "going softly on sin and redemption" is equivalent to proposing another religion with such un-pleasantries eliminated. Not a few claim this is what those who want to reform it want, a Christianity without sin. We have become too frail to bear the truth of our tradition, of what it teaches, of what our real problems are.

Pell's remarks recalled an e-mail I received from a teacher in a Catholic high school. He was assigned a summer-school course and chose to offer one on C. S. Lewis and Tolkien, surely worthy authors. He sent in a prospectus to the program director. The response was that his outline included too many "negative" things, like "good vs. evil, vice and virtue, honor and shame." The students would not react well to such harsh concepts.

Schall was "terrified," as I told the man, that students could not face the most basic of Christian truths at a Catholic school. But it is true that what are called the "negative" elements in Christianity are seldom heard of in our schools, sermons, or universities any more, unless they can be identified as impersonal structural problems. They become issues of diversity, gender, class, or race, but never issues of personal responsibility.

Redemption, it seems, has nothing to do with one's personal sins or deeds. The students are "upset" by core doctrines, or at least some teachers think that they are. "Don't upset the students" becomes censorship. No doubt certain ways of presenting such doctrines can be excessive, but I suspect that is a rare problem today.

When sin is "institutionalized," faith is transformed into a social movement. That is where we deal with the "negative" things today. We work against bad "causes." We work to make the world "better" through judicious selection of movements that "do good." We do not need to attend to ourselves. We do not like to know that our thoughts and deeds have anything to do with something that transcends the growing political correctness in the local culture.

Diversity teaches that whatever anyone does is all right because we act according to how the group we identify ourselves with acts. Multiculturalism, in some of its extreme expressions, teaches that if such is the way they do it in Baluchistan, it must be great everywhere. The only "sin" is that of "prejudice." Prejudice occurs when you acknowledge a truth, but otherwise it seems there are no problems with anything anyone does. Our modern world has just about accepted every classical vice as a virtue or a "right." We fear that we will be "against" something if we label it "evil."

In a visit to Turin, Benedict XVI remarked: "Towards the end of the 19th century, Nietzsche wrote: 'God is dead! And we have killed him'" (*L'Osservatore Romano*, May 2, 2010). Far from disagreeing with this view, Benedict adds: "This famous saying is clearly taken almost literally from the Christian tradition. We often repeat it in the *Way of the Cross*, perhaps without being fully aware of what we are saying." Nietzsche is orthodox!

How is it that we have "killed God"? Surely, it is through our sins and other "negative" things. Thus, if we do not even want to talk about these things, as Tolkien and Lewis do, we will have no conception of what Catholicism is about. We will deny that things we do need attention. Many schools, Catholic ones included, live in an environment in which the early practice of virtue is almost impossible. A friend of mine, who homeschools her son, recently told me that she was grateful to be almost through the "middle-school" period as that was the worst arena morally in most school systems.

How does one deal with *The Lord of the Rings* or *Narnia* if sin, redemption, and their relation to glory cannot be brought up for fear that someone will be "upset"? Chesterton spoke of such aberrations in his time. Literature is taught to prepare the child and adult precisely for the things that will in fact happen. We see what we ought to do by seeing how lives work themselves out when we do not do as we ought.

Catholicism is not a religion that provides a formula for not-sinning. It says, "If you do sin, repent, and go on." Nietzsche himself, I think, was scandalized by Christians who continued to sin. Christ Himself was not so scandalized. He knew we needed doctrine, grace, habit, purpose of amendment, penance, and forgiveness. If we eliminate these things, we invent a religion of perfectionism, not Catholicism.

We tell our young that everything is fine, especially themselves. Just do what others do. Do not judge. Do not distinguish. Do not worry. If something is wrong, it is not your fault. It's the system. You are "ok." Don't worry. Be happy. It would be difficult to imagine worse advice than this as a preparation for what will go on in one's life.

Chapter 20

A Second Look at Hell

CHANCES ARE THAT very few people have ever heard a sermon on hell. It is actually a pretty interesting topic, not at all silly, stuffy, or irrelevant. Hell is found in Scripture. It is also (arguably) found in Plato. It is actually a very useful way to teach or remind us of the importance of our daily actions.

Let us suppose, for the sake of argument, that "hell" does *not* exist. What difference would it make if it didn't? Obviously, if "hell" does exist, we realize its existence makes a difference. If it does not exist, nothing we do makes any difference. Many people who thought that hell did exist have actually lived very evil lives. No matter how we look at it, some pretty bad apples have existed among our kind, however we decide to explain them.

It was once popularly thought that "fear of hell" was a deterrent to bad deeds. At least it was said to minimize the potential damage that "unprincipled" people might inflict on us. But no matter in what age of human history or in what place we look, we will find some astonishingly gruesome deeds perpetrated by fellow members of the human race on each other. We are hard-pressed indeed to explain why this is so. Yet we cannot *not* try to do so, lest we consider reality simply incoherent.

Christianity even suggests that most people, if not most of the time, at least some of the time, do some quite awful and unjustified things. This fact is why one of Christianity's central teachings concerns the forgiveness of sins. So if we think that hell exists, we must, on these grounds, also be able to imagine ourselves suffering in it or because of it. We must also wonder why knowledge of hell did not work better than it did to stamp out what ails us.

Not a few people rebel at this line of thought. "No good god," they fume, "would invent a place of everlasting punishment, no matter what we did!" So if hell exists, they announce, God *cannot* exist. Whether this is a complete disjunction I doubt. It is quite possible to conceive of a universe in which hell is possible because man exists as a free being made by God. His actions and choices have consequences. God could not create man as he is without at least the possibility of hell. Hence, in logic, it follows: "No hell, no man." That was God's real choice in the beginning.

But suppose that neither hell nor God exists. Where does that leave us? It leaves us in a world in which it really does not make much difference what we do. No certain or absolute consequences will or can follow from what we do. But if this lack of seriousness of our actions is the case, it means that our lives are really not important. We are doomed to lives of unending vapidity and meaninglessness. Such a feeling goes against every fiber of our being.

At any moment in my life, however, in any place or in the presence of any others, I can do something (like the things mentioned in the Ten Commandments) that deserves, in justice, some kind punishment, even perhaps eternal punishment. Seen from this angle, the whole world and its inhabitants look very different. How I live suddenly becomes much more central. The old rhetoric about not sinning takes on a new dimension. Perhaps there is a "law" of our being that is not just of our making, one designed to protect our own good.

One thing that I like about the idea of hell is the very exercise of thinking about it.[1] Usually, we never imagine that anything important lies within such ideas, even that they are only imaginary "ideas" with no relation to existence.

It is not as if the human race has not been dealing with this issue almost from the time it began to articulate the implications of what it chose to do with what had been given to it. The most sophisticated thinking regarding hell probably belongs not to Christians but to Plato. We should not be overly surprised that "hell" is a basic topic of probably the most famous philosophical book of our civilization, the *Republic*.

What bothered Plato was whether the world was in fact created in injustice, as it seemed to be. After he observed what happened to his friend and mentor Socrates, namely that he was unjustly executed following a legal trial in the best of cities, he realized that in this world many injustices are not punished and many good deeds are not rewarded. No one could deny this fact.

But, if this was true, what did it mean? It meant that it really made no ultimate difference what we did. If the guilty were not punished and received the same rewards as those who were virtuous—if not better ones—then the world was simply unjust and incoherent. Only if there were an afterlife, if the soul was immortal, could this injustice be requited.

Thus, the doctrine of hell does not arise so much from God as from us. We suddenly realize that without it, nothing we do really makes any difference. It does not "pay" to be either just

---

1. See James V. Schall, "On the Neglect of Hell in Political Theory," in *The Politics of Heaven & Hell*; "The Order of Hell," in *The Order of Things*; "Maritain on the Enigma and Intelligibility of Evil," in *Jacques Maritain: The Philosopher in Society*; "Meditation on Evil," in *The Sum Total of Human Happiness*; "Regarding the Inattentiveness to Hell in Political Philosophy," in *At the Limits of Political Philosophy*.

or unjust. It does not matter. Nothing matters. Most people conclude from such considerations: "Why not be unjust, then?"

John Adams, the second American president, is said to have remarked that "hell is the most essential political doctrine." Why did he say this? Government cannot and ought not to punish all crimes, a view with which Thomas Aquinas agreed. There must be some realization that what the political society does is not the whole explanation of human life.

Government depends on a justice it cannot itself fully realize. Unless we have at least some who are just for the sake of honor and reason, we will live in a jungle. And those who get by with their crimes unpunished cannot be left thinking that therefore there are no consequences for their unjust acts. Governments that profess no belief in hell usually end up making their own version of it present on earth.

Indeed, what often happens is that we cannot bear the notion that the chaos of our lives and societies does not have an intelligible cause. As Benedict XVI suggested in *Spe Salvi*, what we do is transfer the notion of hell from the next world to this world. Political, ecological, or psychological ideologies are proposed to designate the "cause" of evil. Such theories promise to identify these causes and eradicate them. Usually they end up accusing other classes, peoples, religions, or nationalities of creating all human problems. They end up making things worse.

So if we take a final look at hell, we suddenly see that its origin has to do with the freedom in which we are created. If other human beings are as important as we think they are, as they are created to be, it follows that hell indirectly teaches us this basic truth of our dignity. All of us, great and small, are involved in the drama of human existence, our own and that of those we know and live among.

Few people have not seen the wreckage that sins and bad

choices have caused to friends and families. It is not just a question of the great political evils like abortion and bribery, but also of hurts to children, wives, husbands, friends, even enemies. In this sense, I think, hell is a rather helpful to us. Not wanting to end up there is the other side of not wanting to live, or not actually living, disordered lives.

So I am not one of those people who "deplore" the teaching on hell. It is pretty difficult to "think" it out of existence and still end up with a human life that makes any real difference, or even any real reason for existing in the first place.

Chesterton quoted his Calvinist grandfather as saying that he would thank God for his existence "even if he ended up in hell." His point was not that he did not care whether he ended there or not. He meant that the very thought of rejecting existence itself because of the possibility of hell was equivalent to preferring nothing to something.

Once we exist—a gift in the first place—our lives are important enough for us freely to enter the personal drama of wanting to do what is worthy of our existence. Hell is nothing other than the result of our personal refusal, manifested by the way we live our lives, to choose what we ought to be.

The judgment of God is nothing other than the confirmation of our own judging of ourselves. Not even God can "make" us choose to be other than we insist on being. Hell is what is left when we choose to abandon God and His world for ourselves and our self-made world. But unlike Chesterton's grandfather, we do not then thank anyone for our existence, as we have only ourselves to thank for the condition we have arrived at. The whole point of thanksgiving is that you cannot thank yourself. Hell is, as it were, an eternity of trying to do so.

Chapter 21
On Wrath and Anger

CONTRARY TO WHAT we might think, both "anger" and "wrath," accurately understood, are good things. Both words, however, often refer to natural emotion when excessively strong and not guided by reason. Anger indicates a strong reaction. Growing up, we always knew when our fathers were angry.

Wrath depicts something even stronger than anger: the difference between a downpour and a typhoon. The topic of anger comes up in book four of Aristotle's *Ethics*. It is one of those givens in us that needs to be self-governed. We are to be angry in the right time, at the right place, and under proper guidance. People vary in the ease with which this emotion becomes out of control. But it is possible to be either excessively angry or not angry enough.

In scripture, anger and wrath are attributed to God's reaction when He does not like what the Hebrew people are doing. He loves them, but that does not prevent Him from being angry with them. Yahweh always has a good reason for His anger, one of which is to encourage His people to straighten themselves out.

Psalm 88 says: "Your wrath has swept over me." St. Paul tells the Thessalonians: "God has not destined us for wrath but for salvation" (1:5,9). This remark implies that "wrath" might have been a quite legitimate option because of our sins. But the Book of Jonah tells us that "a gracious and merciful" God is "slow to anger" (4:2). Yet this slowness implies: "Don't press too far!" And in Ephesians (4:26–27), we read: "If you are angry, let it be without sin. The sun must not go down on your wrath; do not give the devil a chance to work on you." Here, we find both a sinful and a non-sinful anger. But "wrath" in this context seems to be something we should take care of, even if it is justified. It can lead to much greater problems.

The capacity to be angry is given to us by nature itself. It is part of the whole interrelated "package" of items that constitute *what-it-is-to-be-a-human-being*. Without it, we would be less than we are. We would be crippled, lacking something that ought to be there. *Tell me what makes you angry and I will tell you what you are.* The same point can be made negatively—*Tell me what does not make you angry and I will likewise tell you what you are.*

In the belated publicity about Planned Parenthood selling fetal parts, for instance, many people were angry, even wrathful, on learning of this atrocious commerce. Yet, these same people were often not angry at the evil of abortion itself. That reaction, I suppose, is better than being angry at neither. It shows the greater and lesser evils proportioned to greater and lesser angers.

In my own teaching experience, I would always explain that Aristotle treated both envy and anger in the same general way. Envy always struck me as a much more destructive and prevalent vice than greed, with which it is often compared. Greed is an acquired habit of not controlling our desire for food or money or other material things. Envy, as Aquinas put it, is "sadness" at the good of another. That definition is most perceptive. Unlike drinking or money-gathering, this "sadness" is not a physical thing, though envy and jealousy can indeed change our visage.

Like pride, envy is rather a spiritual thing. Nothing is gained or lost by it. It is an intellectual estimate of another's good that we do not ourselves possess. The problem is not the good that the other really has, but our "sadness" or chagrin at his having it. The point is that he deserves it and we know it.

Pride, as the primary capital vice, is likewise a purely spiritual disorder. Everything is attributed to oneself. This spiritual element is why both angels and men can suffer from pride and envy, whereas angels cannot be greedy in the strict sense.

What about anger and wrath? What now strikes me is that anger also is a spiritual thing. This also explains talk of God's "wrath." It means more than envy. It indicates the need of real "visible" response to evil or disorder, even if we cannot "do" anything about it. For instance, God's anger does not eradicate the free will that originates the disorder to which the anger is directed.

This factor is why we can understand that God's wrath is directed at our world, at our deeds, while we, on our part, blithely go on approving and fostering evil and living disordered lives as "rights" or "diversities." Again, this divine reaction explains the theoretic need of a final judgment on our sins whereby God's "anger" is, as it were, carried out on those who, in their pride and envy, refuse to live in any other world but their own.

Chapter 22

On the Power of Forgiving Sins

"HOW CAN I RESTORE what I have never stolen?" (Psalm 69). The point of this question should be obvious. It's almost a "first principle"; it is too obvious to need further proof. Indeed, if you give back what you did not take, you are not acting justly. You may be acting generously, but you owe nothing. You are not restoring what is "due." To understand things, we must call them by the right names. We ought to make recompense for what we steal. There is no such need for us to give back what we did not steal. These are fundamental issues not just of morality but of intelligence. Anyone can understand them.

"Each tree is known by its yield. Figs are not taken from thorn-bushes, nor grapes picked from brambles." We read this passage in Luke (6:44). Again, these observations seem pretty obvious. Christ turns out to be a pretty good common-sense philosopher. Things are what they are. Thorns are thorns. Figs are figs. If we expect to find figs on thorn-bushes, something is wrong with us, not with the fig tree or thorn-bush. We can tell the difference between them. Reality, *what is*, rules our minds. We call things by their proper names. We say figs are figs and thorns are thorns because that is what they are.

We may be able genetically to improve the quality of figs. We may even produce seedless watermelons or thornless roses, though both seeds and thorns have their reasons for being. All the possibility of genetic modification shows is that the "minds" in nature and our heads have some relation. We still cannot make wine from brambles as we do from grapes. That is why we pick grapes, not thorns. Those soldiers who put the crown of thorns on Christ's head expected that thorns would do what thorns are supposed to do. The fault was not in the thorns, but in those who used them improperly. Our freedom to make wine or enjoy fresh figs depends on our knowing the elementary things about thorns, brambles, grapes, and figs.

Why do I bring up these considerations? In Luke 5, we read of a scene in which certain scribes and Pharisees ask: "Who is this man who utters blasphemy?" This is clearly a pretty serious charge. Blasphemy means to attribute to man or nature what properly belongs only to God. So they ask: "Who can forgive sins but God alone?" Of course, the scribes and Pharisees are perfectly right. No one can do this forgiving on his own.

But in order to understand what is going on in this passage, we first have to know what a sin is. If sin does not mean anything, there is no sense in talking about forgiving it. Next we have to know what forgiveness means. Why is it related to sin? Taking what does not belong to us is a sin. And simply restoring what we did take, while central, still does not get at the heart of what is wrong with stealing. What is crucial is whether we see that "sin" has also something to do with our own characters in light of the divine order. Someone is concerned with what we ought to be, but are not. When we deliberately dis-order ourselves, we are not what we should be. Disorder in the world follows upon disorder in our souls, not the other way around.

Nothing was wrong with the logic of the scribes and Pharisees. Their problem had to do with whether this man standing before them was or was not God. He claimed the very power that they rightly knew belonged only to God. They insisted that

He was not God. However, even when He restores a man's withered hand right before their eyes, they denied what it logically implied. The question thus becomes: "Were they themselves blaspheming because they refused to comprehend the evidence before them?" They were not stupid men. Christ wanted to "make it clear" to them "that the son of Man has authority on earth to forgive sins." This was a divine claim and they knew it. This divine authority applied to them.

So just as we cannot pick grapes from brambles or restore what we did not steal, we cannot forgive sins if no sins exist or if we did not commit any. Even if there are sins, we cannot forgive them if we have no power or authority to do so, just as the fig tree has no power to produce elderberries. Now, I know that we can graft trees of one kind onto another root system. But this does not change the grafted fruit from one kind to another. If I graft an apricot branch onto a black walnut stump, what is produced are apricots, not walnuts.

Thus, we do not change the nature of what sin is when, to avoid its reality, we graft it onto a theory that denies its possibility. Sin is always a choice to be what we ought not to be in some area or other of human life. The classical distinction between mortal and venial sin indicates that some things are worse than others, something everyone recognizes to some degree. First, it is clear that serious disorders exist among us. The whole world is involved in trying to fix what seems constantly to go wrong. What Christianity is about, why Christ comes into the world, however, is firstly so that sins might be forgiven. That is to say, without His presence in the world, they could not be forgiven. The world is filled with disorders with which it does not know how to deal.

We cannot forgive ourselves. We can only be sorry. Sorrow means that we can recognize the distortions that we are responsible for in the world around us. Our power to sin, if we examine it, is ultimately a sign of our transcendent importance. It is also a sign of our freedom. We are so important that our sins reach to the very Godhead. To deny this human worth, which we do by minimizing or eliminating sin, is to reduce our existence to insignificance. It is equivalent to saying that whatever we do makes no difference.

But if our deeds and thoughts were ultimately of little meaning, we would act in very different ways when someone sins against us. We are angry at crimes against ourselves, but not when we do the same thing to others. Our just anger and annoyance would mean nothing if what we did meant nothing. People might say that sin makes no difference. But every thief becomes angry when someone steals from him—and so for every sinner and every sin. The fact is that those who think their lives are meaningless nevertheless do not act that way. Thorns and brambles, as it were, come forth from our sins, not the figs and grapes we expected. This is the nature of things.

Blessed Isaac of Stella was a twelfth-century Cistercian monk. He became the abbot of a small monastery in France. He supported Thomas à Beckett in England. One of Isaac's sermons begins this way: "The prerogative of receiving the confession of sins and the power to forgive sins are two things that belong properly to God alone." What Isaac brings up here is an extension of the principle appealed to by the scribes and Pharisees, namely, that only God can forgive sins. This is in itself perfectly standard doctrine.

So the question becomes whether Christ, who claimed for Himself the power to forgive sins, was God or not. If He was— and, as Benedict XVI argues in *Jesus of Nazareth*, all evidence seems to indicate that He was—then we must ask whether this power of forgiveness is issued to Christ in any old way or is there some orderly means by which sins are prescribed by God to be dealt with. If Christ indeed possessed this power, did he share it with others? If so, was this given to everyone, or were only a few specially commissioned by the Church to do so? Blessed Isaac indicates a twofold step for the forgiveness of sins: a) to "receive the confession" and b) the "power" to forgive the sins that have been confessed. In other words, we have in the world a means whereby our sins, which ought not to have been committed, can be forgiven. This does not mean that our sins have no consequences even if forgiven. We still have to return what we have stolen.

Sins are to be confessed to those who have the authority to forgive them. If I confess to someone with no power to forgive sins, I am not acknowledging Christ's instructions on how to go about it. I am still in my sin. Yet this restriction on whom I am to confess to is for my benefit. We do not, if we are normal, go about telling everyone our sins, boasting about them. This caution does not mean that, once our sins are forgiven, we cannot with some practical wisdom learn something from them, something that may be useful to ourselves or others, if the proper occasion arises. Thus, it was useful, say, for the reformed abortionist, Bernard Nathanson, to tell us of his sins. It is always well to remember that we can learn both from what is good and from what is evil. The knowledge of evil is not itself evil. What is evil is the deliberate doing of it.

Thus, in I Timothy 1, we read: "Nobody should doubt that Christ Jesus came into the world to save sinners." Such a passage serves to clear our minds about what is important. Sins are forgiven in the sacrament. Their forgiveness presupposes their acknowledgement. "The Church is incapable of forgiving any sin," Blessed Isaac continues, "without Christ, and Christ is unwilling to forgive any sin without the Church." Catholics do not maintain that the priest or even the Church, all by itself, forgives sins. What they say, in effect, is that receiving forgiveness requires our following the steps that Christ set down for us. "Whose sins you forgive are forgiven" (John 20:23). This is what we mean by authority. The power to forgive is only given to those designated to possess this power.

"Why did not Christ do it some other, more efficient, way?" we ask. We can imagine other ways that He might have set up. He might have said, for instance, "If you sin, immediately recite Psalm 8." Or, "if you sin take your shoes off and announce your fault in the public square." We can imagine many other ways of proceeding here. But when we think it out, it turns out that the way Christ did operate here was pretty insightful. It requires something on the sinner's part. He is not just left to himself. There must be a judgment about the responsibility for the sin that is not simply one's subjective feeling. He must be told both to "go in peace" and "to sin no more."

Sinners—a group that probably includes everyone sooner or later in one way or another—are to be treated compassionately, as the tradition has always taught and Pope Francis has recently emphasized. But being compassionate does not mean lessening or denying the terrible reality that sin can put in our world. Sins are certain kinds of thoughts, words, and deeds that keep recurring among us. They are at the heart of our own and the world's disorders. To deal with them is why Christ said he came. To call what is sinful a "right," a "duty," or a "freedom" is both to deceive ourselves and to permit the evil to continue in our souls and in the world.

"The Church cannot forgive the man who has not repented; who has not been touched by Christ," Blessed Isaac explains.

"Christ will not forgive the sin of one who despises the Church."
Perhaps the basic reason why the Church is still "despised" is
precisely the same as the reason given by the scribes and Pharisees; namely, its claim to be the locus where sins are forgiven.
Hence, it also claims to be the place where sins are identified.

The Son of Man is the only one "who can forgive sin." These
are Blessed Isaac's final words in his Sermon. They are still true.
We cannot restore what we did not steal. We cannot forgive
what is not in our power to forgive. Christ came to save "sinners," not to abolish the difference been grapes and thorns—
that is, not to tell us that sins are not sins, but to tell us that they
are.

The scribes and Pharisees did not deny that God had the
power to forgive sins. Our world, on the other hand, too often
denies that there are sins to be forgiven. Whatever we do is fine;
it is an expression of our freedom. We often call sins "rights" or
even "duties." Not calling them what they are does not change
them. This denial that sin is sin is probably the one sin that even
Christ said could not be forgiven (Matthew 12:31). All sins can
be forgiven if we repent and freely ask pardon in the Sacrament.

Logically, this denial means that our era is not filled, like an
era of faith, with forgiven sins. Rather it is filled with the consequences of unforgiven sins that we refuse to even call sins. In
the end, we should not forget that God always leaves us our
freedom. He lets the consequences of this freedom work its way
out in our hearts and in our world. The rise and fall of civiliza-
tions reflect how we use or do not make use of the power of forgiving sins that has been given among us.

Chapter 23
The Judgment of God

When one is not aware of *the judgment of God*, when one does not recognize the possibility of hell, of the radical and definitive failure of life; then one does not recognize the possibility and necessity for purification. Then man does not work well on behalf of the world, because in the end he loses his bearings; he no longer knows himself, not knowing God, and destroying the world. All of the great ideologies have promised: We will take things in hand; we will no longer overlook the world; we will create the new, just, correct fraternal world. Instead, they destroyed the world.

Benedict XVI, Address to Roman Clergy, February 7, 2008

The greatest moral challenges headed our way do not, in fact, come from hate-filled fanatics threatening death and destruction. They come rather from well-meaning scientists and technologists offering life, pleasure and enhancement. . . . Human nature itself lies on the operating table, ready for alteration, for eugenic and psychic 'enhancement,' for wholesale redesign. In leading laboratories, new creators are confidently amassing their powers and quietly honing their skills, while on the street, their evangelists are zealously prophesying a post-human future. For anyone who cares about preserving our humanity, the time has come to pay attention.

Leon Kass, Commencement Address,
St. John's College, Annapolis, 2007

SIN IMPLIES a wrong. A wrong is something that must be judged as such. If we cannot say of anything that it is right or it is wrong, we become drifters in the field of morality. If we cannot recognize when we have done something wrong, we cannot be forgiven of its consequence or wrongness. If we cannot judge that anything is right or wrong, it really does not make much difference what we do or say. We cannot form habits of virtue or vice if we do not know what is wrong or whether we did it or not. Human responsibility becomes a long series of protest that "I did not do anything wrong." If the robber did nothing wrong, there is really no robbery. If the adulterer did nothing wrong, there is no adultery. In short, without the capacity to judge we cannot build a coherent world in which we can distinguish good and evil, responsible and irresponsible.

An underlying theme of Benedict's Regensburg lecture is that we are confronted with at least two immediate threats of a world-wide scope.[1] The first is radical Islam, which will not go away. All our naïve pretending that it will naturally disappear is simply based on ignorance. We refuse to grasp how a religion can, after centuries of relative inactivity, suddenly rearm itself to pursue the same goal it had from its beginnings. This goal is the conquest of the rest of the world for Allah by whatever means seem feasible. Very intelligent and aggressive men do conceive that at no time in the modern era has this goal seemed more feasible and attainable by disciplined Islamic movements.

The inner moral weakness of the West is obvious to anyone who cares to look. Two times in the past, at Tours in the eighth century and at Vienna in the sixteenth century, Europe barely escaped Muslim conquest. For their part, the Muslims who pursue these (to them) religious goals see the West as a far easier target today than at any time in the modern era. America and

---

1. See James V. Schall, S.J., *The Regensburg Lecture* (South Bend: St. Augustine's Press, 2007).

especially Europe seem more open to conquest than, say, India or China, objects of earlier Muslim attempted conquests. But these latter can wait. The population decline of the West needs quick replacement, which Islamic immigration is providing.

Benedict's Regensburg lecture, however, was more aimed at the intellectual structure of Europe than at the threat of Islam, in spite of its reputation. The military danger of Islam was not underestimated by the pope. Nor were its intellectual roots in voluntarism left unexamined. Benedict, moreover, knows the background and origins of science, his second area of concern in this lecture. He does not minimize any of the benefits or the genius of scientific method and accomplishment. He is, however, quite critical of this method when it claims that only a system based on matter and mathematics is "scientific," as if there were no spiritual power in the universe or no way to know it. The scientific method itself assumes a spiritual power of knowing.

For a long time, even into early modernity, it was considered that "human nature" would itself be the criterion for establishing the "limits" of science. It was understood that *what man is* by nature cannot and ought not to be experimented with or radically altered. From Hume on there has been a doubt about whether a nature, human or otherwise, exists or can be known; the idea of a limit to human nature has disappeared. Nothing now prevents the elimination of a given human nature as a norm of human worth. Once man himself became an object of his own scientific studies, the very structure of man is called into question. Science becomes not so much a study of *what is* as of what "ought to be," as if what man actually is has no given meaning. We only want to know what we can do. Man himself becomes merely an object of "scientific" improvement as if he is nothing of value in himself. And so the parameters of what it is to be human cannot be defined. Doctors, for instance, no longer clearly state what a patient must do to be cured, but ask "What do you want me to do for you?" If it can be done, we will do it; if not, we will learn how. We are now filled with proposals, as Benedict recalled in *Spe Salvi*, having to do with conception of children, enhancement of bodies or minds, making men women and women men, a single-sexed world, extending life in this world by decades and centuries, cloning, in-vitro fertilization, and other means of bringing human beings into existence apart from a normal family.

We can evidently separate sex and children so that the family experience is totally bypassed, not unlike the proposal in book five of the *Republic*. Other institutions, particularly schools and the state, come to fulfill the family's functions. Why do we want to enact policies that would change our being? Evidently, in part just to see if we can do them, but also because we claim that such changes represent an "improvement" on the original design of a human being. The human good henceforth is to be considered as a scientific project, a work-in-progress. The human good now skips over the whole ethical and social condition of man as we have known him. At the heart of man's good as classically conceived, however, is not something that is done for him by another, but something he must do for himself through his own discipline and free acts.

What is being rejected here? The classical and Christian idea of man accepted the fact that man was by nature good, and in his life should become the kind of being he was meant to be. He was granted a certain limited number of years of life on this earth during which he was to decide his eternal destiny while relating to his fellow citizens in various ways. The human being was to achieve this destiny by practicing the virtues, by understanding what the world and revelation were about, by how he lived, and by what he knew and believed. The central focus was on man's own given dignity. By nature, he was an unfinished project whose life, as it resulted from his choices, was either good or bad. This configuring of himself as good or bad was the most important thing about him. His condition in this regard depended largely on himself. Ultimately, he could not blame someone else for what he turned out to be. The locus of order and disorder in his soul was ultimately in his own free will. This is why he was always seen as subject to judgment, both to identify what is wrong and to reward what is right.

This given nature and destiny implies that man's choices are significant for his either being or rejecting what he ought to be. It is a risk to be a human being. Indeed, it was a risk (and indeed a romance) on the part of God to create man as he was, free. Man did not have to choose what he ought to be, only whether to become what he ought to be. The much-maligned doctrine of hell was about this very issue of the importance of human choice and hence of our relation to God, to others, to the world. Hell is not so much a description of doleful punishment as the logical consequence of what follows when man chooses his own description of himself and what he ought to do.

Hell is an unavoidable possibility if we are really free beings. When we talked about it, we did so to depict the consequences and importance of each of our free acts as they affect us and others. Since He created each human being to be what he was meant to be, God is intimately associated with our acts as they affect others. No free act touches only the one who puts it into effect. Hell thus is always and only the result of a free and intelligent act of a particular finite and rational being. On God's part, man is allowed his own choice. Having made a sinful choice, man sees its logical consequences carried out in his own life unless he confronts his sin through repentance. On his own authority, man, in sinning, specifically rejects the laws of nature and God. God could avoid this only at the cost of making man not to be man.

This consequence of an eternal placing of oneself outside all those who choose God is the other side of the awesome dignity of human independence and autonomy as a real being. God clearly did not create men as patsies or automata. He created something lofty enough to be offered His own inner life, something independent enough to reject it if he so chose. God created the only kind of a being worthy of His love and attention, the only kind of being who could, in grace, properly praise and know Him. Man was created to be happy, in other words, not to be damned.

This is why the primary locus of all drama and all life, public and private, is found within us. This is why we are the most interesting figures in the cosmos. We are the beings in the universe that can reject what we are. We can do this because we are likewise the only beings who are given the gift and choice of accepting to become what we are and are intended to be. We can reject this gift. This is both our freedom and our hell. If we did not have this power, we could not also meaningfully choose glory.

What is characteristic of modern political and scientific thought, however, is that it "confidently" proposes a way to "perfect" man without his having to do or choose anything himself except submit to the new procedures and technology designed, so it is said, to improve him. His ills are now considered to be ultimately external to him and removable. This position is just the opposite of the classic and revelational traditions in which our moral lot is found within us. Disorders, human and moral, can now, it is claimed, be cured by a scientific system.

This transformation of man will be accomplished by the rearrangement of the *polis* or of the family, or, now more immediately, by that of the very human corpus and psyche. Death, which even Scripture says God did not initially intend, is now looked upon, not as the normal, expected, and even welcome end of every human life, but as something that can be postponed if not eliminated, an obstacle to be dealt with. We are told, often without reflecting on what this might mean, that we can look forward to continuous life in this world. This hope that the human life of individuals can be extended for centuries perhaps explains why so few are concerned about falling population growth. Children were once thought necessary to replace dying generations; if we do not die, why do we need children?

Of course, when we imagine what a life of, say, two hundred years might entail, this thinking makes death look rather better than we might have expected. Benedict's *Spe Salvi* treated of this speculation about the scientific "improvement" of the human condition. He concluded that the traditional standard of a life of four-score years and ten, of heaven, hell, death, and purgatory, looks better and better by comparison; on almost every point, orthodox doctrine makes more sense and is more human. We are in fact more likely engaged in "scientific experimentation in creating monsters, not better men." I believe that the author of *Frankenstein*, Mary Shelly, was aware of and frightened by this possibility, as were Huxley and Orwell, the authors of *Brave New World* and *1984*.

The upshot of this reflection is that the primary way to safeguard the human condition as it was given to us as good from the beginning is to rethink the notion of the "judgment of God." Ironically, right thinking about the transcendent order is the only way in which we can protect this world so that it is what it was intended to be. The reason for this is that today scientific thinking proposes to itself a way to achieve the goals of the transcendent order in this world by its own methods. Thus, science can extend our lives indefinitely, we can eradicate evil by political reform, and make ourselves happy by providing everything we want.

Pope Benedict remarked that, in recent years, we have seldom heard serious preaching and discussion of the last things, the things mentioned at the end of the Creed, particularly "the judging of the living and the dead." In part, he attributes this neglect to the abiding influence of Marxism, which claims that the reason for the problems in the world is that Christians are alienated from it. They devote their efforts solely to the transcendent order and thereby neglect this world. Religion is thus the cause of our problems. If only we could forget about anything beyond this world, we could perhaps, even on this earth, build a kingdom suitable for man.

Under the shadow and pressure of this Marxist approach, many Christians shifted their attention to this world. Social justice and temporal problems, rather than spirituality and theology, became the chief concern of such thinkers. Political and economic programs replaced attention to one's soul and its destiny. Ironically, the methods espoused by such activists seldom worked in practice. The application of such ideology to politics often resulted in something far worse than might ever have been imagined. Hell became something of this world in the worst cases. Without judgment, this-worldly hells became even more difficult to explain for our having thought we eliminated the very idea of hell, thereby driving it back as a this-worldly issue.

Of course, as Benedict wrote in both *Deus Caritas Est* and *Spe Salvi*, there is not only room for Christian attention to this world but an absolute necessity for it. The idea that Christians neglected the world was a myth. This life is indeed the place where we work out our destiny, but not without common sense and prudence. What we do for our neighbor is a central criterion for eternal salvation. In this sense, Christianity has a much more realistic and practical view of the world than any of its alternatives. Christianity deals with real people, not abstractions. It believes the world exists with its own order. Christianity also maintains that the supernatural gifts of faith, hope, and charity are directed to what is often lacking in the natural order. Charity, in particular, is the most pressing need of actual people in the real world. We do not need in the place of charity, as the Pope said at the end of *Deus Caritas Est*, only policies and programs run by civil bureaucracies. The human person needs a care and attention that is also personal.

Benedict makes a striking remark about the final fate of those who have caused serious evil in the world and whether they will ultimately have to answer for what they did, in his address of February 7, 2008 to the priests of Rome. "Today, we are used to thinking: 'What is sin?' God is great; he understands us, so sin does not count; in the end God will be good toward all. It's a nice hope. But there is justice and there is real blame. *Those who have destroyed man and the earth cannot sit immediately at the table of God, together with their victims.*" Here he rejects the idea that sin has no consequences and that all will be simply forgiven with no accounting on our part or on God's part. The passage does, as it must, leave open the door for the repentance of even the most hardened sinner. But it by no means makes the great sins simply insignificant acts, as many would like. There is "justice" and "real blame." They have to be acknowledged and accounted for.

What is Benedict driving at here? He is definitely not affirming that everyone will be saved no matter what he does, repentance or not. Rather, he is carving out the grounds upon which our understanding of natural and divine order must rest. The living and the dead will be judged according to their works and their intentions. This is a given found in the very heart of existence. There is also purgatory, whereby those who repent must be further purified before they can see God fully. But first there is judgment. We do not today like the word *judgment*. It means ultimately that we are not the only ones who know and analyze what we do or do not do on an objective basis. A free act is not complete in its being and understanding until it is judged to be what it is.

Even as early as Plato, we have had to ask the question of whether the world was just or not. What is at stake is the world's very intelligibility. This concern for justice means that we have to acknowledge the crimes of men against their fellow men. We cannot "hurt" God, of course, but we can destroy or abuse those He loves, something perhaps even more dangerous. In general, we know what is right and wrong. The Socratic principle upon which our civilization is built is that "it is never right to do wrong." Given a choice between dying and doing wrong, we should prefer death as the lesser evil. The official reason given for the death penalty defines the good dying upholds. Both Socrates and Christ died for the truth of their lives.

If we think out of existence any notion of divine judgment, our acts simply go unrequited or, in the case of good acts, unrewarded. To give them credit, often the famous modern ideologues were horrified at the evil in the world and sought to eliminate and punish those who caused it. They assumed a divine prerogative. But in the processes, they ended up causing greater ills and crimes, since their solutions did not conform to human nature. They supposed that they could use evil to do good. Thus, it is important to recognize that the judgment of God signifies that the right order is not to be tampered with. Sins and disorders will be judged and punished. Otherwise, no ultimate justice can be found. The world is, at bottom, unintelligible when we attempt to explain it only in its own terms.

In *Spe Salvi*, Benedict cites a passage from the Marxist philosopher Theodore Adorno. While Adorno was not a believer, nonetheless he recognized that the accumulation of unpunished sins (and unrewarded benefits) logically leads to the notion of the resurrection of the body. For without this real presence of the real persons involved, the crimes of actual people, or the rewards of the good, could not be dealt with in any ultimate, personal sense. Thus, the doctrine of the judgment of God leads to the doctrine of the resurrection of the body, which is in fact the Catholic position on the matter. The Resurrection of the body is God's granting to man what he is, a complete being of body and soul even in eternity.

How then, we might ask, is this doctrine of the judgment of God an answer to the Marxist charge that Christians are not concerned with this world? It is simply that Christians, by putting things in their right places, take the world much more seriously than do the Marxists. In acknowledging the judgment of God, they are, or should be, much more aware of how we ought to deal with one another. The principles and standards do not ultimately change. And to return to the scientists and indeed to Islam, the judgment of God is not arbitrary. The kind of being we were created to be is a complete person, body and soul. The resurrection of the body restores the original wholeness and opens it to the divine life. But man can also reject his end, which is the point of judgment.

The judgment of God is not merely the affirmation of God about Himself, but the reiteration of the fact that the creature that God made remains by far the best and most exciting reality in earthly creation. This is what the drama of sin and forgiveness is about. We are free. We can choose to accept the gift of what we are, or to reject it. The judgment of God is simply the constant reminder that God intended us to be what we are, persons destined to eternal life, if we choose to accept this destiny.

Chapter 24

A World of Justice, Mercy, and Forgiveness

You forgive the sins of your people when their holy leaders like
Moses sought your compassion. . . .

> Third Intercession, Evening Prayer,
> Common of Pastors, Breviary

But you, God of mercy and compassion, slow to anger, O Lord,
abundant in love and truth, turn and take pity on me.

> Psalm 86:15–16

THE WORLD is not created in justice alone, or mercy, or wrath, or
compassion, or love, or tenderness, but in all of these aspects
together, properly understood and ordered. Hannah Arendt
once remarked that the unique contribution of Jesus to political
life was the concept of forgiveness. What did she have in mind?
She understood the dynamics of justice and injustice. It can be a
never-ending process that does not easily of itself end in agree-
ment.

The vengeance aspect of injustice, the wanting to pay back
more than what is due, can only be stopped when, at some
point, someone forgives the other. Forgiveness is the great contribution of Christ to our understanding of political things. This
forgiveness, however, does not exclude the idea that the one
forgiven may choose not to accept the forgiveness. He need

not—is free not to—do so. The refusal to accept forgiveness, in order to hold onto the feeling that one is wronged, is itself a vice. We can keep alive our sense of being wronged by refusing to acknowledge that a debt is paid.

The dynamic of this book has been impelled forward by the uniqueness of the Christian revelation that initially admonishes us to repent of our sins. Why repent? For the Kingdom of God is at hand. Forgiveness belongs together with justice and mercy. Justice is necessary but harsh. Its general formulation cannot cover all the particular circumstances of actual transactions. Mercy can be a temptation to forgive what is not forgivable. It can become merciless. Forgiveness requires signs of repentance and a willingness to accept punishment. We need to know that the order of soul that our sins violated has been recognized and restored.

A solid doctrinal basis for understanding justice, mercy, and forgiveness does not separate principle from emotion. It understands that the best thing that we do for a sinner, besides (for priests) being instruments in his divine forgiveness in the Sacrament, is to uphold the good, the what-is-right. If we tell the sinner that his sin is no sin, he is locked up in himself without any possibility of escape. The most uncharitable thing we can do to a sinner, as Plato said, is not to punish him, that is, not to tell him that his sin is indeed a sin.

We now live in a relativist world that largely refuses to admit that anything needs to be forgiven because there is nothing to forgive. We are said to be autonomous and to create our own rules. Many lies about reality can be found in our souls and in our culture. These lies too need to be acknowledged, repented of, and forgiven.

A once-famous aphorism says that "to love all is to forgive all." This needs considerable qualification. We can only forgive what is forgivable. We can forgive sins against us. But a sinner is not forgiven until he repents, until he acknowledges that the order of things was disrupted by his act. If God could forgive absolutely everything, which He cannot, it would mean that He could force His will onto our freedom. He would be telling us that our acts made no ultimate difference. He cannot do this, nor does He want to. What can limit God's love and hence His forgiveness is our unwillingness to accept the gift of His love. This love manifests itself as compassionate and merciful when it must deal with a particular disorder that we put into the world by our freedom, by our sins. Love must first deal with the disorder. In this sense, it is called mercy.

In the beginning of this book are found six citations—from the Book of Wisdom, Solzhenitsyn, C.S. Lewis, Chesterton, St. Augustine, and Plato. They foresee and recapitulate what this book is about. Obviously, it is primarily concerned with forgiveness and the ideas and realities that surround it. The Book of Wisdom tells us that the Lord "overlooks" our sins once we acknowledge them, that He loves *all that is*. Solzhenitsyn powerfully teaches us that the division of the world passes through the hearts of each of us.

C.S. Lewis insists that we all recognize a law of nature. But we also know that we break it. Without these two principles, we cannot understand ourselves. Chesterton is right to tell us that we do not want a religion that tells us what we want to hear. We want one that tells us the truth about ourselves. Otherwise, we have no hope of being anything but what we choose to be, not what we ought to be. Augustine speaks of his evil deeds and their punishment. He realizes that God gives us our very being. The good things of creation can, if we are not careful, lead us away from God. But they do not, in the end, satisfy us when we have them. Plato tells us to guard against becoming unjust. But if we act unjustly, we should seek to be punished so that every-one may know that we recognize the evil which we bring upon ourselves and others.

In a remarkable passage in *Deus Caritas Est*, Benedict XVI wrote: "Love—*caritas* [*agape*]—will always prove necessary, even in the most just society. There is no ordering of the State so just that it can eliminate the need for a service of love. Who-ever wants to eliminate love is preparing to eliminate man as such" (27b). This is basically what C. S. Lewis was concerned about in the *Abolition of Man*. While justice is a worthy and noble thing, the origins of totalitarianism lie in the State that takes the works of charity, mercy, and compassion upon itself, usually under the aegis of something called "social justice."

When it comes to forgiveness, Solzhenitsyn was right: "The line separating good from evil passes through every human heart." This human heart is the proper locus for forgiveness and repentance. It is why the Gospels begin with a call to repentance. It is why no crossless Christianity exists. The "judgment" of God is a genuine judgment, as Plato saw. Without this judg-ment, the world could not be just; we could not account for all that happened within it for good or ill. Neither justice alone, nor mercy alone, nor forgiveness alone. The last word is better reflected by those spoken by Augustine to God: "For before I was, you were; I was nothing that you might give me being." In the end, all is gift, including the forgiveness and mercy that we seek. We seek them because we have examined ourselves enough to know that we require both mercy and forgiveness to make our lives worth living.

Appendix

Fifteen Lies at the Basis of Our Culture

To this book on sinning and forgiveness, I have added a short appendix. It is, in fact, a blunt statement of why the need for repentance is so urgent. We lie to ourselves about *what is*, the worst possible thing we can do to ourselves, as Plato said. We have proclaimed that our vices are "rights" and "values" for which we seek fame and honor. Instead of a compassion that justifies the overturning of our reason, we need judgment, forgiveness, penance, and, yes, punishment. Above all, we need to rid ourselves of the lies on which much of our culture is based. The lies speak for themselves. They stand against what I have called "the order of things."[1]

A CULTURE IS A complex composition of the manners, rites, language, laws, ideas, and customs of a people. These elements help account for what a given people hold to be true, or at least valid: how they act to one another, how they build things, how and what they punish and reward, how they think of birth and death.

Some thinkers want to say that truth and falsity are relative to a culture. Whatever the culture does or holds becomes its own absolute in that domain. Any outside revelation or philosophy

1. See James V. Schall, S.J., *The Order of Things* (San Francisco: Ignatius Press, 2007).

may be expected to accommodate itself to the culture, not vice versa. No such thing as a natural law or universal philosophy, whereby one might judge the content of a culture, is acknowledged.

Catholicism has long held that its essential revelation is directed to all "cultures." Whatever is good can be accepted by all. Anything alien to revelation must be modified in light of universal truths. The supposed "neutrality" or autonomy of any culture, however, would make it almost impossible to judge real differences between good and evil, truth and falsity. If such differences do not objectively exist as the same for all cultures, it does not make much difference what we hold or what culture we belong to. In effect, they are all—Western, Muslim, Chinese, Hindu, Byzantine, Japanese, African, Latino, modern, ancient—meaningless.

For those who hold universal principles of reason and revelation, current Western culture, in which the American polity exists, is, in many fundamental matters, based on lies. The devil, interestingly enough, is said to be the "father of lies." This attribution indicates that the devil bases his own life on the lie of his own self-worth. It also means that he can convince human beings—who can imitate him—that the lies they live by are true, not to be challenged or repented of. This "kingdom of lies" is not divided within itself. One lie follows from another. All converge to deny what man and creation are about.

What are these "lies" on which our present culture is based? Each one of them, on examination, denies or violates a principle of reason or a fact of science. But they are all strenuously adhered to as "truth" because they allow us to do what we want. They enable us to avoid responsibilities for our chosen actions. We insist that they are our "rights," our "privileges," or our "liberties."

The first and most obvious *lie* embedded in our culture is that abortion does not kill a specific, actual human being. All evidence shows that abortion does kill such a being. To hold the lie in our souls, we must—as so many do—call it a "right" or a "choice," which allows us to pretend that we know not what we do.

The next lie is that marriage does not necessarily consist in the permanent, legal bond of one man and one woman who together form one flesh, inhabiting a home in which they beget and raise their own children. Any legislation that defines marriage as merely a civil contract between members of the same sex is based on a lie. It denies what marriage is. It denies what is owed to the child: both a mother and a father.

The third lie is that there is a "right" to kill oneself or have others do so for us—euthanasia. Euthanasia is suicide, not an act of compassion or autonomy over ourselves.

The fourth lie is that war is always immoral and never has any legitimate justification. War is never without its evils, but never to allow war's legitimacy in any circumstances whatsoever is to ensure tyranny and ignore the need to defend human good and dignity against those who would destroy it.

The fifth lie is that the poor are poor because the rich are rich. The only way for anyone to become not-poor is for him to learn from those who have learned how to produce wealth sufficient for human needs and well-being.

The sixth lie is that man himself is the chief threat to the well-being of the planet earth. Man's presence on this planet is at least as natural as that of any other being. The well-being of the earth is not more important than the well-being of man. The purpose of the earth is to provide for this well-being, a well-being that knows what the earth is and needs.

The seventh lie is that the earth is over-populated and must drastically reduce its numbers by several billions. The earth, aided by human intelligence and enterprise, can take care of its population. Human well-being is, in fact, more threatened by population decline than over-population.

The eighth lie is that there is no truth. Everything is relative to our individual preferences. Relativism is always self-contradictory. It is a lie to maintain that man cannot know any truth about himself, the cosmos, or God.

The ninth lie is that democracy is always the best form of government. Democracy is that form of government based on a concept of liberty that allows man to do whatever he wants. It generally becomes a form of tyranny of the majority in which whatever the people want is the law and is identified with what is right.

The tenth lie is that the purpose of government is to protect human "rights." As the term is used today, "rights" do not refer to what is due to man. Rather they are rooted in Hobbes's claim that we can do whatever we want to keep ourselves alive and protect what we claim. "Rights" become what the state says and enforces. There is no way to prevent them from becoming tomorrow the opposite of what they are today.

Lie number eleven is that Islam is only a religion of peace. Islam historically expanded by military conquest. Those who die in its wars are considered martyrs. It is considered blasphemy to deny any element of Islam's holy book or tradition. Islam does not tolerate what it does not believe. The Trinity and Incarnation are specifically denied in the Qur'an.

Lie number twelve is that Jesus Christ is not who He said He was, that is, the Incarnate Word of God. All presumed evidence that denies this truth does not bear careful examination.

Lie number thirteen is that Christianity is another religion like all other religions. In fact, it has uniquely reasonable bases for its truths. "Religion" is technically an aspect of the virtue of justice. It attempts to define what man owes to his gods. Christianity is a revelation of a divine Person about who God is and what is necessary for salvation. What it contains is addressed to human reason and does not contradict it.

Lie number fourteen is that sin does not exist, that it can be explained by psychology, determinism, sociology, or myth. It need not be forgiven. The consequences of sin go on whether we like it or not. They become present in the lives of both sinners and those against whom they sin.

Lie number fifteen is that no final divine judgment is possible. This position means that nothing we do makes any ultimate difference. Our lives are hence basically meaningless and of no ultimate worth. But that a final judgment exists is the truth. Since we are free and intelligent, we must give an account and be judged for how we used the gifts given to us.

In suggesting that our culture is founded on these fifteen lies, I do not want to imply that there are no other ones, nor deny the culture also contains aspects of virtue and good. Many people recognize and seek to counteract each of these lies. But in cataloging them, I do argue that lies are connected with each other. One will lead to another once we embrace and live by it. We will find ourselves "being led on," whether we like it or not.

Yet, we need not accept these lies. Eric Voegelin once wisely remarked that "No one needs to participate in the aberrations of his time." But the temptation to do so, to be politically and culturally correct—and it is a temptation—is very great. And as C.S. Lewis noted in *The Screwtape Letters*, our deviation from the good usually does not begin with the large aberrations but with the small ones.

Josef Pieper rightly told us that it is not the "lie" that is the real basis of culture, but "leisure." *Leisure* is the Aristotelian word used to describe what we do when all else that we "need" to do is completed. The implication is that the most important things are not really the economic or political ones that have to do with just living (rather than living well). But to live well, we must think, and in particular think about *what is*, about what we did not make or establish ourselves.

The *things that are* contain their own order, which we must discover lest we deceive ourselves and see only what we want to see. We read in Plato's *Timaeus*: "Now while it is true that anything that is bound is liable to being undone, still only one who is evil would consent to the undoing of what has been well-fitted" (41b). The "lies" that lie at the heart of our culture in fact "undo what has been well-made." We do not acknowledge this disorder because we too often "consent" to the "undoing" of what we are and ought to be.

CPSIA information can be obtained
at www.ICGtesting.com
Printed in the USA
LVOW12s1707150117
521018LV00008B/762/P